# The Crawfish Cookbook

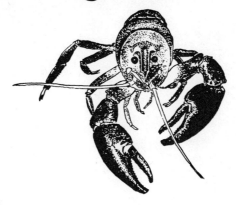

# The Crawfish Cookbook

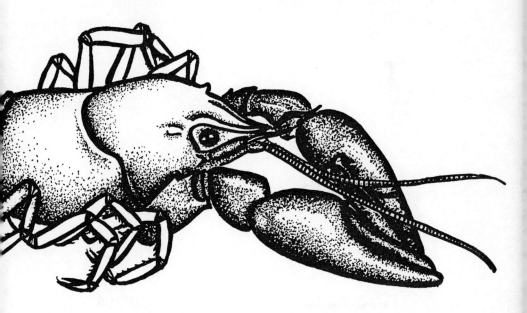

## By Norma S. Upson

**Pacific Search Press**/cooking

International Standard Book Number: 0-914718-21-5
Library of Congress Catalog Card Number: 77-074272
Pacific Search Press, 715 Harrison Street, Seattle, WA 98109
© 1977 by Norma S. Upson. All rights reserved
Printed in the United States of America
Cover and Book Design by Pamela Hoffman
Illustrations by Maxine Morse

To my mother,
who showed us the art of cooking is an act of love.

# Contents

Introduction . . . . . . 9

General Information . . . . . . 11

Ways to Boil Crawfish . . . . . . 15

Appetizers, Cocktail Sauces, and Dressings . . . . . . 23

Soups, Salads, and Sandwiches . . . . . . 41

Crêpes and Quiches . . . . . . 71

Casseroles . . . . . . 77

Entrées . . . . . . 103

International and Southern Entrées and
Deep South Specials . . . . . . 121

Index . . . . . . 151

# Introduction

My family's first reaction to the thought of eating crawdads—as they are called on the river where we live—was "yech!" For they were creepy, cranky, crawly critters living deep and secretive lives in the bottom ooze and debris.

Second thoughts and a little research gave us the insight we needed to revolutionize our thinking. Crayfish, crawfish, crawdads, or mudbugs are first cousins to one of our favorite fish foods, the New England, or American, lobster of the East Coast. They are, in fact, a form of *freshwater lobster!* This was the revelation that changed our "yech" attitude toward them to a speculative "hummmmmm." A little further practical research soon proved crawfish worthy of an enthusiastic "mmmmmmmm!" It isn't everyone on earth who has lobster growing in the backyard, but my household is blessed. We can catch them, cook them, experiment with them, study them, and, of course, eat them anytime we want to.

Crayfish, or crawfish as they are called in many areas of North America, are found on all continents of the world. Streams, lakes, and ponds abound with them. They vary in size from the minuscule quarter-inch variety to the whopping eight-pounder found in Tasmania.

Not only are crayfish more numerous and accessible than their seagoing cousin, but they are just as delicious and provide the same amount of protein per pound, plus more phosphorus than any other fish flesh.

In Europe the crayfish is considered a gourmet food and is used with the same reverence and discrimination as the esteemed lobster; but for those of us who live where there is a more bountiful supply, all sorts of wonderful recipes have been found to utilize them. For any person who has access to fresh water, the crayfish provides healthful, gourmet food for practically no money. Or, for those who are not so blessed, better fish markets sell crayfish for less per pound generally than the costly seagoing lobster.

Our friends and neighbors on the river supply their needs by building or buying traps in which they place bait—fish, meat, or chicken parts. They lower the traps, and once or twice a day they remove the "dads" to holding tanks in which they undergo a cleansing process. (See General Information for details of preparation prior to boiling.) When enough have been caught and cleansed to provide a bountiful meal, the crayfish are popped into boiling water. Once boiled, they are ready to use in any one of a hundred or more different ways.

We have used crawfish cooked "plain" for a "crawfish feed," as appetizers or hors d'oeuvres, and as entrées. There are nine or ten ways we have found in which to boil them, and because each way is in its own manner delicious, it is impossible to say which is the best. We have smoked them using various brines and spices and woods, and each method has given us a smoked fish product superior to any other we have ever eaten. We have marinated them in all manner of ways and found them delicate and exciting in color and taste.

As for using the crawfish as an ingredient for the main course, it is unbeatable in elegance and variety. For breakfast, an omelet using crawfish either as a secondary ingredient or in a creamy sauce is the perfect way to start a Sunday or holiday. For lunch, in soups, salads, crêpes, or patties, there is no finer ingredient. And for dinner, the many casseroles, sauces, stuffings, and soup-bowl dishes containing crawfish are superior to any other fish dish we have ever tried.

The traditional Creole, Cajun, or southern crayfish dishes will always be favorites, for they, like all fine foods, have a long and honored history of pleasing the eye, nose, taste, and stomach. However, there are other less obvious and nonregional recipes, which will delight anyone who enjoys cooking and eating shellfish.

It is because we have found crayfish to be versatile, inexpensive, interesting, and delicious that we have prepared this book to share the joys of this humble crustacean, this first cousin to the mighty American lobster, with gourmet and gourmand alike.

*Bon appétit!*
N.S.U.

# General
# Information

Crawfish generally thrive in clean water of fifty-five to sixty-six degrees Fahrenheit in states on the Gulf of Mexico and the Mississippi River; the range is about ten degrees lower in the Northwest. But because these crustaceans eat flesh food as well as vegetation and adapt readily to varying water conditions, the crawfisherman would be wise to check any stream, pond, or lake for possible pollutants. Your state fish and game department or your local board of health is happy to provide anyone with information on the purity of any body of water.

Even though water may be clean and all conditions healthful, it is wise to treat crawfish with utmost care after catching them. They *are* fish and therefore among the most perishable of foodstuffs. Keep them chilled until they are cooked. Live crawfish become dormant and can safely be kept between thirty-five and forty degrees Fahrenheit. The sooner they are cooked after their removal from water, the safer and better they will be.

Like lobster, crab, and shrimp, which belong to the same order as the crayfish (Decapoda), these bottom feeders are usually cleaned to remove any impurities or objectionable taste. Our method of cleaning is simple, for we live where there is ample water and space to provide a holding or keeping tank into which we pop our crawfish immediately after removing them from our traps. Then we feed them fresh vegetable scraps, which our local grocer would ordinarily discard. Lettuce leaves, carrot and beet tops, and so forth are put into the tank for the crawfish. Any river carrion they have eaten is automatically replaced by wholesome, sanitary food.

It is a matter of preference as to how one chooses to clean crawfish after they leave the holding tank and are on their way to the table. Our method is to remove the entrails by twisting the central fan in the tail and pulling out the entrails, or central alimentary canal. Next we pop them into a bucket of salt water (one-half cup salt to one gallon water). Salt removes tiny parasites that feed on the mossy algae growing on the shell of the crawfish. (These parasites in no way affect the flesh within.) After being immersed in the salt water, the crawfish are clean and ready to be boiled by one of the methods described at the beginning of the recipes.

Some of our friends wait until after the crawfish are cooked to remove the entrails. Others feel that boiling them directly from the river is sufficient to clean them. If you opt to cook them with their entrails intact, before eating or using them, remove the dark vein that runs through the body in just the same way as you would before eating shrimp or lobster.

Many gourmets prefer to eat whole cooked crayfish in this manner: Twist off the tail section, removing it from the body. Remove a couple of sections of the shell to expose the meat. Simultaneously grasp the meat and press the tail, and the meat will easily be extracted. A flick of the nail will remove the dark vein on the crawfish and it is ready to eat, dipped in hot butter or in the sauce of your choice.

One of the mistakes the novice crawfish cook makes is overboiling. Overboiling toughens the flesh and produces a bland, tough, stringy meat. Just as with cooking lobster or crab, crawfish should never be overcooked or water-soaked.

However, while researching recipes, we found that the *time* allowed to cook crawfish varies greatly from area to area. In Louisiana, for instance, one recipe for boiling, printed by the Louisiana Center for Wetland Resources, calls for a boiling time of fifteen minutes and soaking the crawfish for twenty minutes after that! (This is due to the species of crawfish used.) Compare this to the general preparation instructions one receives in the Willamette Valley in Oregon: Boil a mere two to five minutes and *never* soak a crawdad. The best conclusion we could reach is that it would be wise to consult a local home economist. The differences in boiling time depend on the variety, the thickness of shell, and/or the size of the crawfish.

Basically there are three things to remember when cooking crayfish, regardless of kind or location: (1) Use only live, clean crawfish. (2) Kill instantly by dropping into boiling water. (3) Keep them chilled until used.

To figure out the equivalents in measuring crayfish, one must again take into consideration the *kind* of crayfish being used. The Oregon variety we tested (*Pacifastacus leniusculus*) generally proved out this way:

> One pound liveweight equals one cup meat (using tails and claws).

Twelve medium-sized crawfish (six to seven inches long in shell) are sufficient for one serving.

One cup crawfish meat generally serves from two to six, depending on other ingredients.

In its brochure on crayfish farming and crayfish recipes, the Cities Service Oil Company of Louisiana suggests six pounds liveweight equals one serving. We could find no information on how many crayfish tails would be needed to make one cup of tail meat; however, we have tried to transpose all of the amounts of crayfish called for in recipes into cups. The rule of thumb might be twelve to twenty medium crayfish equals one cup—*generally!*

Crawfish "fat," or "butter," is found in the body of the crawfish above the tail section. It is a golden green substance, the consistency of paste, and is used to enrich many dishes or as a spread on crackers or toast points for the more adventuresome palate.

Because crayfish have only recently come into their own as a commercial shellfish, economists and cooks have not recorded amounts needed in recipes except in a few traditional recipes. We found that almost every lobster recipe could be transposed into one using crawfish, which is not surprising when one realizes that crawfish *are* the freshwater cousins of lobster.

# Ways to Boil Crawfish

Each crawfish lover seems to know the *best* way to cook them—all different! Here are some variations. (See General Directions for cleaning crayfish.)

## I

*(This is the method of boiling we found most prevalent in the Northwest. Use this "plain" method to prepare crayfish for use in other dishes in this book unless otherwise directed.)*

SALT    ratio of ½ cup to
WATER    1 gallon
LIVE CRAWFISH
COLD WATER

Add salt to water and bring to a boil. Drop in crawfish; bring water back to brisk boil and boil 2 to 3 minutes until crawfish turn bright red. Remove immediately from heat and chill by immersing quickly in cold fresh water or by pouring cold water over crawfish (this facilitates shell removal). Eat or refrigerate. Clean before eating.

## II

SALT    ½ cup
PICKLING SPICE    2 tablespoons
WATER    1 gallon
LIVE CRAYFISH
COLD WATER

Add seasonings to water and bring to a boil. Drop in crayfish. Boil 2 to 3 minutes until bright red; quickly place in cold water to cool. Clean.

## III

VINEGAR     2 tablespoons
SALT     ½ cup
PICKLING SPICE or FINES HERBES (optional)     2 to 4 tablespoons
WATER     1 gallon
LIVE CRAYFISH
COLD WATER


Add vinegar and seasonings to water. Bring to a boil. Drop crayfish into pot and boil 2 to 3 minutes; quickly plunge into cold water. Clean.


## IV

(Here's how the Finns enjoy crawfish.)


SALT     ½ cup
FRESH or DRIED DILL     2 tablespoons
WATER     1 gallon
LIVE CRAWFISH
COLD WATER


Add salt and dill to water and boil several minutes. Add crawfish, boil for 2 to 3 minutes, and plunge into cold water. Drain, clean, and eat.

## V

ALLSPICE      4 tablespoons
SALT      4 tablespoons
SUGAR      1 tablespoon
WATER      1 quart
LIVE CRAYFISH
WHITE WINE or SAKI      1 cup

Add allspice, salt, and sugar to water and bring to a boil. Add crayfish. When they turn red, remove from heat and cool. Place crayfish and wine in bowl; cover and allow to steep overnight in refrigerator. Clean. These are excellent appetizers.

## VI

SALT      ½ cup
WATER      1 gallon
LIVE CRAYFISH
COLD WATER
BEER      to cover crayfish

Add salt to water and bring to a boil. Drop in crayfish and boil 2 to 3 minutes. Remove from pot and cool quickly. Place in bowl and cover with beer. Refrigerate overnight. Clean. Use as appetizers.

# VII

SALT      ½ cup
WORCESTERSHIRE SAUCE      3 tablespoons
BAY LEAVES      3
GARLIC CLOVE      1, diced
WHOLE CLOVES      1 teaspoon
GROUND NUTMEG      1 teaspoon
ALLSPICE      2 teaspoons
CAYENNE      ½ teaspoon
MEDIUM ONION      1, diced
WATER      4 quarts boiling
BURGUNDY WINE      1 cup or
(JUICE OF 2 LEMONS      in 1 cup WATER)
LIVE CRAWFISH      5 dozen

Put spices and onion in cheesecloth bag; place in boiling water. Boil about 2 minutes. Pour in wine. Drop in crawfish. Boil 2 to 3 minutes. Chill and clean before serving.

# VIII

(This recipe is for crawfish three to four inches long.)

LIVE CRAWFISH
WATER      boiling

Break crawfish at junction of body and tail. Pull out meat in tail. Meat will remain in 1 piece; entrail and shell will separate. Steam quickly 2 or 3 minutes until meat turns pink. Clean. Serve or refrigerate.

## IX

(Here is the Cajun method for cooking crawfish for "plain eating," as reported by James W. Avault, Jr., Professor of Fisheries, Louisiana State University, Baton Rouge, Louisiana.)

"Fill a twenty-gallon pot about two-thirds full of water. Add two boxes of crab boil [a spice combination] and two twenty-six-ounce boxes of table salt. Cut up and add a few lemons and sweet onions if available. While waiting for the water to boil, throw in some new potatoes. When the water boils, you can either remove the potatoes or leave them in until done. Corn-on-the-cob can be cooked in the boiling water for five minutes, if you have some handy. If not, proceed to boil your crayfish. Add about twenty pounds of live crayfish, or whatever the pot will hold, to the boiling water. Make sure all the crayfish are covered with boiling water. When the crayfish are added, the water will stop boiling. When it resumes boiling, allow the crayfish to boil for fifteen minutes. Then cut off the fire and let the crayfish soak for twenty minutes." Serves 6 to 8.

*See also* Louisiana Crawfish Feed.

# Appetizers,
# Cocktail Sauces,
# and
# Dressings

# CRAWFISH COCKTAIL

LETTUCE LEAVES     6
LETTUCE     2 cups finely shredded
CRAWFISH MEAT     1½ cups, cooked and cleaned
ANY COCKTAIL SAUCE     see index
PARSLEY     to garnish
LIME SLICES     6

Arrange lettuce leaves in 6 cocktail glasses. Add ⅓ cup shredded lettuce in each. Place crawfish meat on top. Cover with cocktail sauce. Sprinkle with parsley and serve with slice of lime. Serves 6.

.     .     .     .     .

Crawfish are omnivorous and will eat just about anything. They even eat one another! (A soft, newly molted crawfish is vulnerable to this fate.) They live mostly on plant life, but given their preference, they choose animal matter.

# SMOKED CRAWFISH

## LIVE CRAWFISH

Cook 2 to 3 minutes until they turn bright red. Wash and devein.

*BRINE*

| | |
|---|---|
| WATER | 1 quart |
| SALT | ½ cup |
| SUGAR | ½ cup |

| | |
|---|---|
| MACE | to taste |
| DILL | to taste |
| ALLSPICE | to taste |
| GARLIC | to taste |
| ONION SALT | to taste |
| MAPLE FLAVOR | to taste |
| BAY LEAVES | to taste |
| WHITE PEPPER | to taste |
| PICKLING SPICE | to taste |

Combine brine with choice of seasonings. Cure crawfish in brine for 2 hours—longer for saltier taste. Remove crawfish and rinse under tap water. (Brine can be kept for further use.) Place crawfish on paper towels to absorb excess moisture. Allow to dry in air for 1 to 2 hours. Place in smoker for ½ to 2 hours (the time it takes to use 2 pans of hickory sawdust). Refrigerate until used as appetizers.

# MARINATED CRAWFISH

VEGETABLE OIL    ½ cup
OREGANO    ½ teaspoon
BASIL    ½ teaspoon crushed
SALT    ½ teaspoon
PEPPERCORNS    6
PARSLEY    1 tablespoon chopped
RED WINE    ½ cup
CRAWFISH    36, washed, cooked, and cleaned
LEMON SLICES    to garnish

Heat oil in large frying pan. Add all ingredients except crawfish and lemon. Cook slowly for 2 minutes. Add crawfish, cover, and bring to a boil. Lower heat and cook slowly for 5 minutes. Garnish with lemon slices and serve immediately. Serves 6 to 8.

.    .    .    .    .

The two most popular varieties of crawfish grown commercially in Louisiana are the red swamp and white river crawfishes. The white river variety is the larger of the two, but the red swamp is noted for its generous offering of yellow gold butter (fat), which is highly prized in crawfish dishes.

# CRAWFISH IN COURT BOUILLON

## (A Gourmet Cocktail or Appetizer)

ONION    ⅓ cup chopped
CARROTS    ½ cup diced
CELERY    ⅓ cup chopped
PARSLEY SPRIGS    2
BUTTER    2 tablespoons, melted
PEPPERCORNS    6
WHOLE CLOVES    2
BAY LEAF    1
SALT    2 tablespoons
WATER    2 quarts
VINEGAR    2 tablespoons
LIVE CRAWFISH    36 to 40
LETTUCE, ENDIVE, or WATERCRESS    as needed
LEMON or LIME SLICES    to garnish

Cook vegetables in butter, browning slightly (about 5 minutes). Put spices into cheesecloth bag and tie. Add water, vinegar, and spices to pot; simmer 30 minutes. Bring to a boil and add crawfish. (Crawfish simmered for 2 to 3 minutes in court bouillon is a gourmet appetizer or cocktail.) Cook quickly and cool quickly; clean. Serve crawfish on bed of lettuce and garnish with lemon. Serve with crackers and a cocktail sauce (see index). Serves 6 to 8.

# TOASTY CRAWFISH APPETIZER

MAYONNAISE 1½ tablespoons
DRY MUSTARD ½ tablespoon
LEMON JUICE ½ tablespoon
CRAWFISH MEAT ½ cup cooked and cleaned
WHITE BREAD SLICES 6, toasted
PARMESAN CHEESE ⅛ cup grated
BREAD CRUMBS 1 tablespoon

Combine mayonnaise, mustard, lemon juice, and crawfish. Remove crusts from bread. Spread crawfish mixture on each slice of toast. Combine cheese and bread crumbs. Sprinkle over each slice. Cut each slice into 6 pieces and place on broiler pan 3 inches from heat. Broil for about 2 minutes or until brown. Makes 36 appetizers.

# CRAWFISH PARTY DIP

CRAWFISH TAILS 1 pound (1 cup meat), cooked and cleaned
CREAM CHEESE 1 8-ounce package
HORSERADISH 1 teaspoon
LEMON JUICE 1 teaspoon
ONION JUICE 1 teaspoon
CHILI SAUCE ¾ cup
WORCESTERSHIRE SAUCE 1 teaspoon

Chop crawfish meat fine. Mash cream cheese thoroughly. Blend in crawfish. Add other ingredients. Chill. Serves 8 to 10.

# CRAWFISH CHUNKS

ONION    ½ tablespoon grated
BUTTER    ⅛ cup, melted
FLOUR    ⅛ cup
MILK    ½ cup
EGG YOLK    1, beaten
WORCESTERSHIRE SAUCE    ¼ teaspoon
SALT    ⅛ teaspoon
PEPPER    dash
CRAWFISH MEAT    ½ cup cooked and cleaned
DRY BREAD CRUMBS    ⅜ cup
OIL    for deep frying

Sauté onion in butter. Blend in flour. Add milk gradually. Cook until thick, stirring constantly. Combine yolk, Worcestershire sauce, and seasonings. Blend with onion mixture and crawfish. Chill for 1 hour. Using a teaspoon, shape mixture into small balls. Roll in bread crumbs. Deep fry until brown. Serve with a sauce (see index). Makes 30 appetizers.

.   .   .   .   .

Crawfish tails are one of the favorite baits used by fishermen to catch trout, steelhead, and bass.

# MOCK MOUSSE DE CREVETTES

CRAWFISH MEAT     1½ cups cooked and cleaned
ARMAGNAC BRANDY     ¼ cup
DIJON MUSTARD     1 tablespoon
GERVAIS CHEESE*     1 6-ounce package
TRUFFLES or RIPE OLIVES     1 tablespoon finely chopped
FRESH DILL     1 tablespoon chopped
LEMON JUICE     1 tablespoon
SALT and PEPPER     to taste

Combine all ingredients in blender and whirl at high speed until smooth. Sides of blender will have to be scraped 2 or 3 times during blending process. Chill. Use on fresh vegetables or on French rusks as a spread. Ample for 6.

*French cream cheese

# EGGS STUFFED WITH CRAWFISH

EGGS     6, hard-cooked
MAYONNAISE     ⅓ cup
CELERY     ½ cup finely chopped
DRY MUSTARD     1 teaspoon
SALT     ½ teaspoon
CRAWFISH MEAT     ¾ cup cooked and cleaned
PAPRIKA     to garnish
PARSLEY or RIPE OLIVES

Cut eggs in half lengthwise. Remove yolks and mash them. Combine with mayonnaise. Add celery, mustard, salt, and last of all, crawfish. Mix well. Fill egg whites. Sprinkle with paprika. Garnish with sprig of parsley, bit of crawfish meat, or ring of sliced olive. Serve as an appetizer, as an entrée, or as a garnish for potato salad, tossed salad, or vegetable salad. Makes 12 stuffed eggs.

.   .   .   .   .   .

A champion Louisiana crayfish eater once consumed over thirty pounds of crayfish in one sitting! That was the liveweight of the crayfish. He actually ate about five pounds of tail meat!

# FAMILY FAVORITE

GARLIC SALT   ¼ teaspoon
LEMON JUICE   ¾ cup
CELERY   3 tablespoons chopped
SALT   ½ teaspoon
TABASCO SAUCE   3 dashes
CAYENNE   dash
HORSERADISH   ⅛ teaspoon

Combine all ingredients. Chill. Serves 6.

# RIVER HOUSE CRAWFISH DRESSING

MAYONNAISE   ½ cup
SOUR CREAM   2 tablespoons
CATSUP   2 tablespoons
GREEN PEPPER   2 tablespoons chopped
GREEN ONIONS   2 tablespoons chopped
HORSERADISH   2 tablespoons
EGGS   2, hard-cooked and diced
RIPE OLIVES   2 tablespoons chopped
PEPPER   dash
SALT   dash

Combine all ingredients. Chill. Pour over cocktail or salad. Serves 6.

# CREOLE COCKTAIL SAUCE

| | |
|---|---|
| CORNSTARCH | 2 tablespoons |
| COLD WATER | 2 tablespoons |
| HOT WATER | ¼ cup |
| TOMATO PASTE | ¼ cup |
| TOMATO SAUCE | ⅔ cup |
| SALT | 2 teaspoons |
| PEPPER | dash |
| CLOVES | pinch |
| SUGAR | 1 teaspoon |
| TABASCO SAUCE | to taste |
| BACON SLICES | 3, diced |
| ONION | ⅓ cup finely chopped |
| CELERY | ½ cup finely chopped |
| GREEN PEPPER | ⅓ cup finely chopped |

Combine cornstarch and cold water. In large pot, blend cornstarch paste, hot water, tomato paste, tomato sauce, seasonings, and sugar. Add Tabasco sauce. Cook over low heat for 20 minutes. In frying pan cook bacon until crisp and remove from pan. In bacon drippings add onion, celery, and green pepper. Cook for 5 minutes. Add tomato mixture. Cook over low heat for 10 minutes. Add crumbled bacon pieces. Chill. Makes 3 cups.

# TART COCKTAIL SAUCE

CHILI SAUCE    ¾ cup
CELERY    ¼ cup finely chopped
LEMON JUICE    1 tablespoon
HORSERADISH    1 tablespoon
SALT    ½ teaspoon
TABASCO SAUCE    dash

Combine all ingredients. Chill. Serves 6.

# ROCKY POINT SAUCE

LEMON JUICE    2 tablespoons
CATSUP    ¼ cup
CUCUMBER    2 tablespoons grated
ONION    2 tablespoons minced
SALT    ¼ teaspoon
CAYENNE    dash

Combine all ingredients. Chill. Serves 6.

## DRAWN BUTTER SAUCE

BUTTER      ⅓ cup
FLOUR       4 tablespoons
WATER       2 cups boiling
SALT        ¼ teaspoon

To make a roux, melt 4 tablespoons butter in a double boiler; add flour, and stir. Gradually add water, stirring constantly until sauce comes to boiling point. Simmer until thick and smooth. When ready to serve, add salt and remaining butter in small bits, beating constantly. Serves 6 to 8.

## A VERY DELICATE SAUCE

SALAD DRESSING      1 cup
LEMON JUICE       3 tablespoons
SESAME SEEDS       ½ cup toasted

Mix dressing and lemon juice together. Dip crawfish in mixture and then in sesame seeds. Or can be used as dressing with sesame seeds as topping.

# CRAWFISH SAUCE

RAW CRAWFISH TAIL MEAT     1 cup cleaned
COURT BOUILLON or FISH STOCK     2 cups
BUTTER     4 tablespoons, melted
FLOUR     3 tablespoons
LIGHT CREAM     ⅓ cup
SALT and PEPPER     to taste
LEMON JUICE     1 teaspoon

Cook crawfish meat in court bouillon for 2 to 3 minutes. Remove crawfish and reserve broth. In saucepan blend butter with flour; add broth gradually, stirring until thick. Add cream, salt, and pepper. Before serving, add crawfish sprinkled with lemon juice. Serve over fish, green salad, or crawfish cocktail. Serves 4 to 6.

## MUSTARD BUTTER

BUTTER    ½ cup, melted
LEMON JUICE    1 tablespoon
SALT    ¼ teaspoon
PREPARED MUSTARD    2½ teaspoons

Combine all ingredients and beat until sauce is thick and cool. Serve chilled. Makes about ⅔ cup.

## MAÎTRE D'HÔTEL BUTTER

BUTTER    ½ cup
LEMON JUICE    1 tablespoon
PARSLEY    1½ tablespoons chopped
SALT    ¼ teaspoon
PEPPER    ¼ teaspoon

Cream butter with remaining ingredients. Chill and serve. Makes about ¾ cup.

# PINK MAYONNAISE

MAYONNAISE or SALAD DRESSING    1¼ cups
CHILI SAUCE    ⅓ cup
VINEGAR    2 tablespoons
PARSLEY    1 tablespoon chopped
ONION    1 teaspoon grated
WORCESTERSHIRE SAUCE    1 tablespoon
HORSERADISH    1 teaspoon
CAYENNE    dash

Combine all ingredients and beat with rotary beater or wire whisk. Refrigerate. Makes about 2 cups. Keeps well and is delicious on salads and cocktails.

.   .   .   .   .

The species of crayfish called mud crayfish (*Orconectes immunis*) is found predominately in the Midwest and South in swamps, muddy-bottomed ponds, and so forth, and because of its muddy taste, is not edible. It is, however, highly sought for use as bait because of its paper-thin shell. It is sometimes regionally called the paper-shell crab. This crawfish burrows deep during droughts and is thus able to survive dry weather and extreme heat and cold that might otherwise destroy it.

# BEURRE BLANC

WINE VINEGAR    ¼ cup
SHALLOTS    1 tablespoon chopped
PARSLEY    1 tablespoon chopped
SALT and PEPPER    to taste
BUTTER    ½ cup, melted


In saucepan combine all ingredients except butter. Simmer until mixture is reduced to ½ original amount. Beat in butter until sauce is foamy. Serve hot. Makes about 1 cup.

# Soups, Salads, and Sandwiches

# MULTNOMAH CHANNEL CHOWDER

BACON SLICES     6, diced
ONIONS     1 cup sliced
CELERY     ½ cup chopped
GREEN PEPPER     ½ cup chopped
TOMATOES     1 1-pound, 12-ounce can
WATER     1 quart boiling
CHICKEN BOUILLON CUBES     2
SALT     2 teaspoons
PEPPER     ¼ teaspoon
BAY LEAF     1
THYME     1½ teaspoons
POTATOES     3 cups cubed
CRAWFISH MEAT     1 cup cooked and cleaned
PARSLEY     2 tablespoons chopped
PLAIN or SEASONED CROUTONS

In 6-quart Dutch oven or kettle, sauté bacon until crisp. Remove bacon and set aside. Add onions, celery, and green pepper. Sauté over low heat until tender. Add tomatoes, water, and bouillon cubes. Bring to a boil. Add seasonings. Cook 5 minutes. Add potatoes; cook 20 minutes or until potatoes are barely tender. Add crawfish to top; do not stir. Reduce heat and simmer gently in covered kettle until all flavors blend (about 10 minutes). Add parsley. Serve garnished with croutons. Makes 3 quarts or about 10 servings.

# CRAWDAD SOUP FOR SUMMER

CRAWFISH MEAT    2 cups cooked and cleaned
BUTTERMILK    1 quart
CUCUMBERS    1½ cups peeled and chopped
GREEN ONION    ½, chopped
GREEN PEPPER    ½, chopped
RADISHES    6, thinly sliced
SALT    1 teaspoon
PEPPER    ¼ teaspoon
FRESH DILL    to garnish

Combine all ingredients except dill in large bowl. Cover and refrigerate at least 12 hours. Serve in chilled bowls; garnish with dill. A good make-ahead dish for hot weather. Serve with hot French bread and white wine. Serves 4 to 6.

.    .    .    .    .    .

The California crawfish (*Pacifastacus klamathenis*) is considered gourmet food. However, most California crawfish are marketed for bait. Anglers of the state prefer crawfish bait to any other for catching the large and wily brown trout.

# CRAWFISH CHOWDER

LIVE CRAWFISH    15 pounds
FLOUR    ½ cup
COOKING OIL    8 tablespoons
MEDIUM ONIONS    2, chopped
WATER    6 to 8 cups
GREEN ONION TOPS    ¼ cup chopped
PARSLEY    to taste
CRUSHED RED PEPPER    ¼ teaspoon or to taste
BLACK PEPPER    to taste
SALT    to taste
EGGS    6, hard-cooked

Cook, shell, and clean crawfish, removing tail meat. In a heavy pot make a roux of flour and oil; brown thoroughly. Add onions and crawfish tail meat. Simmer over low heat for 10 minutes. Add water and cook for 30 minutes. Add onion tops, parsley, and seasonings. Slice eggs in half. Serve chowder in bowls; top each serving with egg. Serves 4 to 6.

# CRAWFISH STEW I

SHORTENING    ½ cup
FLOUR    ⅔ cup
LARGE ONION    1, chopped
GARLIC CLOVES    2, chopped
CELERY STALK    1, chopped
CRAWFISH MEAT    3 cups cooked and cleaned
WATER    1 pint
SALT and PEPPER    to taste

In a heavy pot heat shortening. Add flour and stir until brown. Add onion, garlic, celery, and then crawfish. Stir until stew looks shiny. Add water. Simmer 20 minutes. Season to taste. Serves 6.

.    .    .    .    .

Crawfish bodies are metameric (segmented). They are covered by an exoskeleton of chitin (horny organic component). The body has joined appendages, an open circulatory system, and a reduced body cavity.

# CRAWFISH STEW II

| | |
|---|---|
| LIVE CRAWFISH | 10 pounds |
| CRAWFISH FAT | 2 cups |
| ROUX or COMMERCIAL MIX | to taste |
| ONIONS | 2 cups chopped |
| CELERY | 1 cup chopped |
| WHOLE TOMATOES | ½ 16-ounce can |
| COOKING OIL | 1 cup |
| WATER | 1 pint |
| SALT and PEPPER | to taste |
| CAYENNE | to taste |
| WATER | 1 gallon |
| GREEN ONION TOPS | ½ cup chopped |
| PARSLEY | ½ cup chopped |
| STUFFED SHELLS | 12 (see Crawfish Bisque Manchac) |

Cook and clean crawfish, removing tail meat and crawfish fat; set aside. To the roux add onions, celery, tomatoes, oil, and pint of water. Cook in a heavy pot over medium heat for 30 minutes. Season to taste and set aside. Boil crawfish fat in gallon of water. Season with salt and pepper. Add onion tops, parsley, and roux mixture. Cook over low heat for 1 hour. Add crawfish tail meat. Bring to a boil for 15 minutes. Just before serving, add stuffed shells. Serve with rice. Serves 4 to 6.

# CRAWFISH BISQUE MANCHAC

Manchac is a small town in Louisiana noted for its fabulous shellfish food. It is located between Lake Pontchartrain and Lake Maurepas. This recipe and the Crawfish Stew II recipe originated there.

| | |
|---|---|
| FRESH CRAWFISH | 10 pounds |
| CRAWFISH FAT | 2 cups |
| BUTTER | ½ cup |
| ONIONS | 2 cups chopped |
| CELERY | ½ cup chopped |
| SALT and PEPPER | to taste |
| CAYENNE | to taste |
| STALE BUNS | 8, soaked in water |
| EGGS | 6, beaten |
| STALE BREAD | ¼ loaf, crumbled |
| GREEN ONION TOPS | ½ cup chopped |
| PARSLEY | ¼ cup chopped |

Parboil crawfish. Peel and clean crawfish tails. Clean and save body shells for stuffing. Save crawfish fat. Put butter, onions, celery, and most of crawfish fat into heavy pot. Cook uncovered over medium heat until onions are translucent, stirring constantly. Season with salt, pepper, and cayenne. Add soaked buns. Mix well. Add eggs. Add stale bread. Chop crawfish tails and add to mixture. Add green onion tops and parsley. Add a little more crawfish fat and stock to moisten, if needed. Stuff shells with mixture and serve with Crawfish Stew II (see index). Serves 4 to 6.

# COLUMBIA RIVER BOUILLABAISSE

| | |
|---|---|
| BASS FILLETS | 2 pounds |
| PERCH OR CRAPPIE FILLETS | 1 pound |
| SALAD OIL | ¼ cup |
| BUTTER | 3 tablespoons |
| GARLIC CLOVE | 1, crushed |
| ONIONS | 2 cups sliced |
| GREEN PEPPER | 1 cup sliced |
| CELERY | 1 cup chopped |
| LEEKS | 2, chopped |
| SALT | to taste |
| PEPPER | ¼ teaspoon |
| THYME | 1½ teaspoons |
| SAFFRON | ⅛ teaspoon |
| BAY LEAF | 1 |
| TOMATOES | 1 1-pound can |
| TOMATO PURÉE | 1 10½-ounce can |
| DRY WHITE WINE | 1 cup |
| CRAWFISH MEAT | 2 cups cooked and cleaned |
| WATER | as needed, boiling |
| PARSLEY | 2 tablespoons chopped |

Cut fish fillets into serving pieces. Set aside. Heat oil and butter in heavy saucepan to medium heat. Add garlic, onions, green pepper, celery, and leeks. Stir until tender. Add salt, pepper, thyme, saffron, bay leaf, tomatoes, tomato purée, and wine. Cook 5 minutes. Add fish fillets. Bring to a boil; then reduce heat, cover, and simmer for 15 minutes. Add crawfish meat. Simmer for 10 minutes. If mixture is too thick, add small amount of boiling water. Serve sprinkled with parsley. Makes 2 quarts or 6 to 8 servings.

# SUNDAY NIGHT SALAD

CRAWFISH MEAT      2 cups cooked and cleaned
STUFFED OLIVES      2 tablespoons sliced
HERB-GARLIC DRESSING (PREPARED)      ½ cup
WHOLE NEW POTATOES      1 1-pound can, drained and sliced
FRENCH-STYLE GREEN BEANS      1 16-ounce can, drained
INSTANT MINCED ONION      1 teaspoon
CUCUMBER      ¾ cup thinly sliced
SALT      ⅛ teaspoon
SUGAR      ⅛ teaspoon
WHOLE BABY BEETS      1 8¼-ounce can, drained and chilled
CRISP LETTUCE      as needed
CARROT      ½ cup grated
TOMATO      1, quartered
EGGS      3, hard-cooked and sliced
SWEET and DILL PICKLES      to garnish

Mix crawfish with olives and 2 tablespoons dressing. Cover and refrigerate. Toss potatoes and green beans with ¼ cup dressing and onion. Cover and refrigerate. Sprinkle cucumbers with salt and sugar and refrigerate. On large platter arrange crawfish mix, potato mix, and beets in mounds over a bed of lettuce. Garnish with cucumber, carrot, tomato, eggs, and pickles. Serve with additional dressing if desired. Serves 6.

# COLD CRAWFISH SALAD

CELERY    ½ cup chopped
CRAWFISH MEAT    1 cup cooked and cleaned
LETTUCE LEAVES
WHITE WINE DRESSING    see below

Toss celery and crawfish meat together lightly. Mound on lettuce and pour White Wine Dressing over salad.

## WHITE WINE DRESSING

DRY WHITE WINE    ¼ cup
WHITE VINEGAR    1 tablespoon
SALT    ½ teaspoon
PEPPER    ⅛ teaspoon
ONION    1½ teaspoons grated
PEANUT OIL    ⅓ cup

Combine all ingredients in jar and shake vigorously to mix well. Makes ½ cup dressing.

. . . . .

Crawfish are eaten by fish, bullfrogs, reptiles, birds, mink, raccoon, people, and by each other.

# PROVENÇALE CRAWFISH SALAD

WHITE BEANS   1 16-ounce can, drained
RICE   3 cups cooked
CRAWFISH MEAT   1½ cups cooked and cleaned
GREEN PEPPER   ½ cup chopped
RED ONION   ½ cup chopped
GREEK or RIPE OLIVES   ¼ cup chopped
OLIVE OIL   3 tablespoons
LEMON JUICE   ¼ cup
WINE VINEGAR   1 tablespoon
SALT   1 teaspoon
BLACK PEPPER   ¼ teaspoon
LETTUCE LEAVES
EGGS   hard-cooked and sliced
TOMATO WEDGES   to garnish

Rinse beans under cold water. Allow to drain well. Combine with rice, crawfish, green pepper, onion, olives, olive oil, lemon juice, vinegar, and seasonings. Chill salad several hours. Fill lettuce-lined bowl with salad and garnish with eggs and tomatoes. Serves 6.

. . . . . .

Crawfish are also called crayfish, mudbugs, crawdads, grass crabs, and paper-shell crabs.

# HOUSEBOAT SUPPER SALAD

FROZEN ARTICHOKE HEARTS     1 9-ounce package
CLEAR FRENCH DRESSING     6 tablespoons
CRAWFISH MEAT     2 cups cooked and cleaned
LARGE TOMATOES     2
CRISP LETTUCE     4 cups finely shredded
SHARP CHEDDAR CHEESE     ¼ cup shredded
RIPE OLIVES     to garnish

Cook artichokes as package directs and cool. Slice in half. Toss with 3 tablespoons French dressing. Refrigerate 3 hours. Gently toss crawfish with remaining French dressing and refrigerate 3 hours. Remove stem end of tomatoes and halve crosswise. Place 1 cup lettuce in each of 4 salad bowls and place a tomato half on each bed of lettuce. Arrange artichoke hearts on tomato halves. Mound crawfish on top of artichokes. Pour dressing over each. Sprinkle with cheese and garnish with olives. Serves 4.

.   .   .   .   .   .

On the head of the crayfish are one pair of antennae and one pair of antennules. These are used for balance and sensory perception.

# CRAWFISH AND CUCUMBER QUICKIE SALAD

CUCUMBERS     1 cup sliced medium thin
SALT     ½ teaspoon
WHITE VINEGAR     3 tablespoons
SOY SAUCE     1½ tablespoons
SUGAR     2 tablespoons
SESAME SEEDS     1 tablespoon, toasted
CRAWFISH MEAT     1 or 2 cups cooked and cleaned
LETTUCE

Sprinkle cucumbers with salt. Let stand about ½ hour. Press out moisture. Combine vinegar, soy sauce, sugar, and sesame seeds. Pour over cucumbers. Add crawfish. Toss lightly. Chill and serve on lettuce. Serves 4.

. . . . . .

How to Catch a Crawfish with a Line:   Using a long piece of string or line, tie bait on the end and lower it into the water. (Chicken necks, backs, and bacon rind seem to be most successful.) When there is a tug on the line, slowly and gently draw the bait to the surface. The crawfish will cling to the bait. When the crawfish is brought to the surface, pop it into a net or bucket. When home, place it in a holding tank until ready to cook.

# CRAWFISH ARNAUD

RED WINE VINEGAR    ¼ cup
CREOLE MUSTARD    3 tablespoons
SALT and PEPPER    to taste
PAPRIKA    1 tablespoon
OLIVE OIL    ½ cup
GREEN ONIONS    4, finely minced
CELERY HEART    ½, finely minced
CRAWFISH MEAT    from 36 to 40 crawfish, cooked and cleaned
LETTUCE

Mix vinegar, mustard, salt, pepper, and paprika. Then add oil, beating thoroughly. Add onions and celery; mix well. Pour sauce over crawfish and marinate 4 or 5 hours in refrigerator. Serve cold on lettuce. Makes enough for 8 to 12 servings.

. . . . . .

There are crawfish farms in Missouri, Texas, Mississippi, and Arkansas, but most of the crawfish come from Louisiana, which produces them in such numbers that there are commercial crawfish processing plants licensed and regulated by the Louisiana board of health to provide safe and sanitary conditions.

## ROCKY POINT BEAN AND CRAWFISH SALAD

VINEGAR     ½ cup
SUGAR     ½ cup
SALAD OIL     ½ cup
ONION     ½ cup chopped
CELERY     ¾ cup sliced
GREEN PEPPER     ½ cup chopped
SHELLIE BEANS     1 16-ounce can
CUT WAXED or YELLOW STRING BEANS     1 16-ounce can
CRAWFISH MEAT     2 cups cooked and cleaned
SEASONINGS     to taste

Combine first 6 ingredients and mix well. Add drained beans and crawfish to dressing, tossing lightly. Season to taste. Chill at least 1 hour before serving. Serves 4 to 6.

.   .   .   .   .   .

Crayfish vary in size from the American dwarf crayfish, which is one inch long, to the Tasmanian crayfish, which reaches a weight of eight pounds!

# CRAWFISH CRUISING SALAD

ELBOW MACARONI    1½ cups
CRAWFISH MEAT    2 or 3 cups cooked and cleaned
CELERY    ¾ cup sliced
GREEN ONION    ⅓ cup chopped
MAYONNAISE    ¾ cup
PICKLE RELISH    2 tablespoons
SALT    ½ teaspoon
PEPPER    dash
EGGS    3, hard-cooked and sliced
PARSLEY    to garnish

Cook macaroni according to directions on package; drain and cool. In a large bowl mix crawfish, macaroni, celery, and green onion. Combine mayonnaise, relish, salt, and pepper. Pour over macaroni mixture. Refrigerate for several hours. Garnish with eggs and parsley. Serves 6.

.  .  .  .  .  .

The eyes of a crawfish are compound, stalked, and movable.

# WILLAMETTE RIVER SALAD

MEDIUM POTATOES   7
MEDIUM ONION   1
ITALIAN-STYLE SALAD DRESSING   1 bottle
SALMON MEAT   1 cup cooked
CRAWFISH MEAT   1 cup cooked and cleaned
LETTUCE   as needed
FRESH DILL   1 tablespoon
EGGS   hard-cooked and sliced
TOMATO WEDGES   to garnish

Peel and cook potatoes; slice into ¼-inch slices. Peel onion and cut into ⅛-inch slices; separate into rings. In a shallow dish arrange potato slices and onion rings in alternate layers. Pour ¾ cup salad dressing over all, cover, and refrigerate for 3 hours. Break up salmon; toss with crawfish in small bowl. Pour remaining dressing over fish. Refrigerate covered until serving time. To serve, alternate potato and onion slices with fish mix on bed of lettuce. Sprinkle dill over top and garnish with eggs and tomatoes. Serves 6 to 8.

# BROILED TOMATO-CRAWFISH SALAD

TOMATOES      6 (about 3 inches in diameter)
WHOLE, PITTED RIPE OLIVES      1 3½-ounce can, drained
MIXED SEASONING      1 teaspoon
BASIL LEAVES      1 teaspoon
WHITE PEPPER      ¼ teaspoon
LETTUCE      as needed
CREAM CRAWFISH DRESSING      see below
PARSLEY SPRIGS      to garnish
PAPRIKA      to garnish

Cut each tomato into 4 wedges. Place in shallow greased baking dish, skin side down. Add olives. Sprinkle with mixed seasoning, basil, and pepper. Broil 5 inches below broiler element for 10 minutes. Place on crisp lettuce. Pour dressing over tomatoes. Garnish with parsley and paprika. Makes 8 3-wedge servings.

# CREAM CRAWFISH DRESSING

CREAM CHEESE      1 3-ounce package
SOUR CREAM      1 cup
BLUE CHEESE SALAD SEASONING      1 tablespoon
CHIVES      1 teaspoon chopped
SALT      ¼ teaspoon
CRAWFISH MEAT      1½ cups cooked and cleaned

Beat cream cheese and sour cream to blend. Add all other ingredients except crawfish. Fold in crawfish. Serves 8.

# SAUVIE ISLAND SALAD

PEELED WHOLE POTATOES    1 1-pound can
FROZEN ARTICHOKE HEARTS    1 9-ounce package, cooked
CRAWFISH MEAT    1 cup cooked and cleaned
SWEET GHERKIN PICKLES    ¼ cup sliced
DRESSING    see below
SALAD GREENS

Cut potatoes into 4 slices each. Toss artichokes, potatoes, crawfish, and gherkins together gently. Pour dressing over mixture. Cover and refrigerate until ready to serve. Serve on a bed of salad greens. Serves 6 to 8.

## DRESSING

SOUR CREAM    ¾ cup
CLEAR BOTTLED FRENCH DRESSING    ¼ cup
FRESH DILL    1 tablespoon
BLACK PEPPER    ⅛ teaspoon

Mix all ingredients together. Shake well before pouring over salad. Makes 1 cup dressing.

# SLICED TOMATO CRAWFISH

CELERY     1 cup very finely chopped
EGGS     2, hard-cooked and finely chopped
ONION     1 tablespoon chopped
CRAWFISH MEAT     1 cup cooked and cleaned
HORSERADISH     1 teaspoon
CHIVES     1 tablespoon chopped
MAYONNAISE     1 cup
LEMON JUICE     ¼ cup
GARLIC SALT     1 teaspoon
PEPPER     ¼ teaspoon
TOMATO SLICES     18
LETTUCE LEAVES     6
PARSLEY SPRIGS     to garnish

Combine celery, eggs, onion, and crawfish meat; set aside. Blend horse-radish, chives, mayonnaise, lemon juice, garlic salt, and pepper. Combine mayonnaise mixture with crawfish mixture and chill. Arrange 3 tomato slices on each lettuce leaf. Top with crawfish mixture and garnish with parsley. Serves 6.

. . . . . .

Crawfish, shrimp, crab, and lobster all belong to the order of Decapoda because all have ten legs (five pairs).

# CRAWFISH REMOULADE

CRAWFISH MEAT     3 cups cooked and cleaned
TARRAGON VINEGAR     ½ cup
CATSUP     2 tablespoons
HORSERADISH MUSTARD     4 tablespoons
SALT     1 teaspoon
CAYENNE     ½ teaspoon
GARLIC CLOVE     1, finely chopped
SALAD OIL     1 cup
ONION     ½ cup minced
CHIVES     ¼ cup chopped
CELERY     ½ cup finely chopped
LETTUCE LEAVES     6
EGG SLICES     to garnish
PARSLEY     to garnish

Chill crawfish thoroughly in refrigerator. Mix next 10 ingredients in a bowl to make dressing and allow to "set" for at least 1 hour. (Can be made ahead and refrigerated for several days.) Place mounds of crawfish on lettuce leaves. Top with dressing and garnish with egg and parsley. Serves 6.

.  .  .  .  .  .

Thomas H. Huxley's *The Crayfish,* published in 1880, is a classic zoological study of crawfish and is still considered the best reference work.

# OVERNIGHT PARTY SALAD

SANDWICH BREAD    1 long sliced loaf
EGGS    4, hard-cooked
ONION    1, finely chopped
CELERY    1 cup finely chopped
MAYONNAISE    3 cups
CRAWFISH MEAT    4 cups cooked and cleaned
LETTUCE    as needed
TOMATO WEDGES    to garnish
OLIVES    to garnish

Remove crusts from bread and cube. Chop eggs fine. Combine bread, onion, and eggs. Cover tightly and refrigerate overnight. Next day, combine next 3 ingredients with bread mixture. Serve on lettuce. Garnish with tomatoes and olives. Serves 10 to 12.

. . . . . .

Most commercial crayfishermen tend their traps morning and evening and market their catches once a week.

# CRAWFISH LOUIS

ICEBERG LETTUCE    1 head, thinly sliced
CRAWFISH MEAT    2 cups cooked and cleaned
EGGS    4, hard-cooked
CHIVES    ½ cup finely chopped
LOUIS DRESSING    see below
PARSLEY SPRIG    finely chopped

Arrange lettuce on 4 salad plates or in salad bowls. Mound ½ cup crawfish meat on each lettuce portion. Rice eggs over crawfish and sprinkle chives over eggs. Refrigerate. When ready to serve, pour Louis Dressing lavishly over each salad and garnish with parsley. Serves 4.

## LOUIS DRESSING

MAYONNAISE    1 cup
CHILI SAUCE    ¼ cup
SMALL ONION    1, finely grated
PARSLEY SPRIGS    3 or 4, finely chopped
CAYENNE    dash
HEAVY CREAM    ⅓ cup

Combine mayonnaise and chili sauce. Add onion, parsley, and cayenne. Whip cream until it holds its shape. Mix gently with chili sauce mixture to form dressing. Makes about 2 cups.

# FRUITED SEAFOOD SALAD

WHITE MEAT FISH    2 cups cooked and flaked
CRAWFISH MEAT    2 cups cooked and cleaned or
(CRAWFISH MEAT and CRAB MEAT    1 cup each)
SMALL ORANGES    3, peeled and sectioned
CELERY    ½ cup chopped
GREEN PEPPER    ½ cup chopped
RICE    1 cup cooked
CURRY DRESSING    see below
LETTUCE    as needed
COCONUT    ½ cup, toasted or
(SLIVERED ALMONDS    ½ cup)

Mix first 6 ingredients together. Add Curry Dressing and toss lightly. Chill until serving time. Serve on lettuce; garnish with coconut. Serves 8 to 10.

## CURRY DRESSING

MAYONNAISE    ½ cup
SOUR CREAM    ½ cup
CURRY POWDER    ½ teaspoon
LEMON PEEL    ½ teaspoon grated
LEMON JUICE    2 teaspoons

Combine all ingredients, mixing thoroughly. Makes 1 cup.

# JESSIE'S CRAWFISH ROLLS

CRAWFISH     1½ cups cooked and cleaned
SHARP CHEDDAR CHEESE     2 cups grated
EGGS     3, hard-cooked
SWEET PICKLE RELISH     ⅓ cup
GREEN ONION     ⅔ cup finely chopped
MAYONNAISE     approximately 1 cup, to moisten
SWEET PICKLE JUICE     a little
SANDWICH ROLLS     4 to 6

Blend first 5 ingredients with mayonnaise and pickle juice. Spread generously on sandwich rolls and broil. Serves 4 to 6.

# HOT AND CHEESY CRAWDAD ROLLS

CRAWFISH MEAT     2 cups broken pieces cooked and cleaned
PROCESSED AMERICAN CHEESE     1 cup shredded
ONION     ¼ cup chopped
CELERY     ¼ cup chopped
CASHEWS or ALMONDS     ¼ cup
SALAD DRESSING     ¼ cup
LEMON JUICE     1 teaspoon
PEPPER     ⅛ teaspoon
HAMBURGER ROLLS     4, split

Mix all ingredients but rolls; spread mixture on rolls. Wrap rolls in foil and bake at 350° until cheese melts. May be baked on charcoal broiler 4 inches from coals, turning frequently to prevent burning. Serves 4.

．　．　．　．　．　．

In Oregon crawfish are abundant. The state ranks second to Louisiana as a commercial producer. The Willamette River and Columbia River flood plains produce the major portion of commercially caught crawfish. The subspecies most often found in Oregon are *Pacifastacus leniusculus trowbridgii* and *Pacifastacus leniusculus leniusculus.* The season for personal crawfishing is open yearlong, but the commercial season in the Northwest is limited to the period from early spring to late fall.

# OPEN-FACED CRAWFISH-AND-CHEESE SANDWICH

CRAWFISH MEAT     1½ cups cooked and cleaned
MEDIUM WHITE SAUCE     2 cups
BUTTER
TOAST     6 slices
AMERICAN CHEESE     6 slices
PAPRIKA

Add crawfish to white sauce. Butter toast and cover with slice of cheese; place on cookie sheet and broil until cheese melts. Pour crawfish mixture over slices and sprinkle with paprika. Return toast slices to oven for hot open-faced sandwich; broil to golden brown. Serves 6.

# CRAWFISH PICNIC PATTIES

CRAWFISH MEAT    2 cups cooked and cleaned
CELERY    ½ cup finely chopped
MAYONNAISE    ⅓ cup
ONION    2 tablespoons minced
CHILI SAUCE or PICKLE RELISH    2 tablespoons
LEMON JUICE    1 teaspoon
BREAD CRUMBS    ¼ cup
SALT, PEPPER, and MARJORAM    to taste
COOKING OIL
HAMBURGER or HOT DOG BUNS    4
COLESLAW    as desired

Stir together first 6 ingredients. Shape into 4 patties to fit buns. Season bread crumbs with salt, pepper, and marjoram and coat patties with bread crumbs. Cover bottom of skillet with oil and heat to medium temperature. Fry patties about 5 minutes, turning to brown on both sides. Serve on buns on which you have spread your favorite coleslaw. Serves 4.

. . . . . .

The first description of a North American crawfish is said to have been written by Fabricius in 1798.

# Crêpes
# and Quiches

# DINNER CRÊPES

(The easiest and most impressively elegant recipe on the river!)

CRÊPES    4
PREPARED WHITE SAUCE    1 cup
PEPPER    ¼ teaspoon
DRY MUSTARD    ¼ teaspoon
CRAWFISH MEAT    2 cups cooked and cleaned
TOPPING    see below

Make 4 large crêpes, using favorite "from scratch" recipe or crêpe recipe on mix package. Mix next 4 ingredients and use ¼ to fill each crêpe. Roll, placing loose edge on bottom of greased pan. Cover with topping. Bake 10 minutes at 375° or until topping is brown.

## TOPPING

HEAVY CREAM    ¼ cup, whipped
SWISS CHEESE    ¼ cup grated
PARMESAN CHEESE    ¼ cup grated

Combine ingredients and spread over crêpes.

. . . . . .

The last five pairs of appendages on the abdomen of a crawfish are called swimmerets. There is a fanlike tail, which forms the posterior section of the abdomen. The central section of this fan is twisted and then pulled in order to remove the entrails before or after cooking.

72

# LUNCHEON CRÊPES

CRÊPES    8
CRAWFISH MEAT    2 or 3 cups cooked and cleaned
WHITE WINE or LEMON JUICE
ASPARAGUS or BROCCOLI SPEARS    8, cooked until tender
WHITE SAUCE
CHEDDAR or SWISS CHEESE    shredded

Prepare 8 crêpes, using your own recipe or mix package directions. Heap crawfish on crêpes; sprinkle lightly with wine; top with spears and roll crêpes, placing loose edge on bottom of greased pan. Cover crêpes with white sauce and cheese. Place under broiler until cheese bubbles. Serve immediately. This dish also freezes nicely.

. . . . . .

In the eastern states, the northern crawfish (*Orconectes virilis*) grows to a length of five to six inches. It thrives in both warm-water and cold-water streams and lakes and can be found from Wisconsin, where it is fished commercially, to Maine.

# CURRIED CRAWFISH QUICHE

BUTTER or OIL
PIE SHELL     1 9-inch shell, baked*
CRAWFISH MEAT     1 cup cooked, cleaned, and drained
LIGHT CREAM or EVAPORATED MILK     1½ cups
ONIONS     2 tablespoons minced
CHIVES     2 teaspoons chopped
CURRY POWDER     ½ teaspoon
SALT     ½ teaspoon
EGG YOLKS     2
EGG     1
MONTEREY JACK or SWISS CHEESE     ½ cup grated

Lightly butter the bottom of prepared pie shell. Spread crawfish meat over bottom of shell to distribute evenly. Heat cream to scalding. Add onions, chives, curry powder, and salt. Beat egg yolks and egg until light. Stir in most of cheese. Gradually add hot mixture to egg mixture, stirring constantly. Ladle over crawfish. Sprinkle with remaining cheese. Set on baking sheet on lowest shelf in oven. Bake at 375° for 25 minutes or until filling has set (use knife test as you would for custard). Cool 10 minutes before serving. Cut into wedges. Serves 4 to 6.

*Note: Any favorite pie shell may be used. *Do not prick crust* to keep bubbles from forming. Instead, pour dried beans or rice over foil or waxed paper placed in bottom of pie shell to keep pastry from puffing while baking. Remove foil and beans or rice when pie shell is done.

# CRAWDAD QUICHE

PIE SHELL     1 9-inch shell
BUTTER or MARGARINE     2 tablespoons
MEDIUM ONION     1, chopped
FRESH MUSHROOMS     1 cup sliced
CRAWFISH MEAT     1 cup cooked and cleaned
EGGS     3
MILK     ½ cup
CHEDDAR CHEESE     2 cups shredded

Bake pie shell 10 minutes at 400°. Heat butter in skillet. Sauté onion and mushrooms until just tender. Spoon into pie shell. Spread crawfish over vegetables. Beat eggs in small bowl until frothy; add milk. Sprinkle cheese over crawfish. Pour egg mixture over crawfish. Bake at 400° for 15 minutes. Lower temperature to 350° and bake 20 minutes longer (or until knife withdraws clean from quiche). Allow to stand about 5 minutes before serving. Serves 4 to 6.

.     .     .     .     .

Crawfish have five pairs of walking legs. The first pair are much bigger than the others and are used to catch and to crush food. These large pincers are called chelae. *Chela* is, incidentally, the name given to the disciple of an Indian (Hindu) religious teacher!

# Casseroles

# CRAWFISH DUCHESSE

SHALLOTS or MILD ONION     2 tablespoons finely chopped
MEDIUM MUSHROOMS     8, sliced
BUTTER     ½ cup
CRAWFISH MEAT     2 cups cooked and cleaned
LEMON     1, juice
DRY WHITE WINE     1 cup
MILK     1 cup
FLOUR     2 tablespoons
SALT and PEPPER     to taste
EGGS     2, yolks and whites separated
CREAM or EVAPORATED MILK     1 cup
MASHED POTATOES     3 cups lightly whipped
CHEDDAR CHEESE     grated or shredded

Sauté shallots and mushrooms in ¼ cup butter. Add crawfish and simmer gently for 5 minutes. Add lemon juice and wine and simmer another 5 minutes. Add milk and bring to a boil. In a bowl, mix flour with ¼ cup butter. Combine with crawfish mixture to thicken sauce. Season to taste. Lower heat—*do not boil.* In a separate bowl beat egg whites frothy. Combine with cream. Blend with crawfish mixture and pour into shallow casserole.

*Duchesse:* Beat egg yolks lightly; blend into potatoes. Place in pastry bag and decorate edge of casserole dish. Sprinkle whole dish with cheddar cheese.

Bake at 350° for 1 hour or until potato is browned. Serves 6 to 8.

# CRUSTY CRAWFISH

SEASONED DRY BREAD CRUMBS     1½ cups
BUTTER     ¾ cup, melted
GREEN ONION     3 tablespoons finely chopped
MILK     1½ cups
FLOUR     ¼ cup sifted
CRAWFISH MEAT     1½ to 2 cups cooked and cleaned
PREPARED MUSTARD     1 teaspoon
SALT     ¼ teaspoon
GARLIC SALT     1 tablespoon
RED PEPPER FLAKES     ⅛ teaspoon
SOUR CREAM     ½ cup
LIME SLICES     to garnish

Broil bread crumbs until brown and crisp. Place into greased casserole with ½ cup melted butter. Press crumbs and butter over sides and bottom of casserole. Sauté onion in remaining butter until tender; gradually add milk and flour, stirring constantly, cooking until smooth. Add crawfish, mustard, salt, garlic salt, and red pepper to mixture and cook until heated thoroughly. Remove from heat and blend in sour cream. Pour mixture into casserole and bake at 375° for 10 or 15 minutes until bubbly. Remove from oven and let stand 5 minutes. Garnish with lime slices. Serves 6.

# DEVILED CRAWFISH

BUTTER    4 tablespoons
FLOUR    2 tablespoons
CHICKEN BROTH or BOUILLON    1 cup
WORCESTERSHIRE SAUCE    1 teaspoon
TABASCO SAUCE    8 drops
CRAWFISH MEAT    2 cups cooked and cleaned
EGGS    2, hard-cooked and chopped
ONION    1 tablespoon grated
GREEN PEPPER    2 tablespoons chopped
SALT    ¼ teaspoon
BREAD CRUMBS    2 cups
DRY BREAD CRUMBS    ½ cup

Melt 2 tablespoons butter and blend in flour. Add liquid gradually. Cook, stirring constantly until thick and smooth. Add Worcestershire sauce and Tabasco sauce. Combine all ingredients except remaining butter and dry bread crumbs. Place in a well-greased casserole (or in 6 individual casseroles). Top with butter and dry bread crumbs. Bake in moderate oven (375°) for about 15 to 20 minutes or until brown. Serves 6.

.    .    .    .    .    .

Once I found a tiny crawfish no longer than one-quarter inch in the mouth of a fresh-caught perch. The little crayfish was perfectly formed, very active, and was a lovely transparent silver, reflecting every color in the rainbow.

# HELYN'S CASSEROLE

CRAWFISH MEAT     1 cup cooked and cleaned
TUNA     1 7-ounce can
POTATO CHIPS     2 cups crushed
MUSHROOM SOUP     1 10½-ounce can
MILK     ¼ cup
BREAD CRUMBS (optional)     buttered
PAPRIKA     optional

Mix thoroughly all ingredients except last 2. Place mixture in a greased casserole. Top with bread crumbs and paprika if desired. Bake at 350° for 30 minutes. Serves 6.

.   .   .   .   .   .

In Louisiana crawfish are commercially stocked in ponds in late May or June. Brood stock is "planted" at the rate of fifty to sixty pounds per acre, depending on the amount of vegetation and the number of native stock present. This crop of crawfish can be harvested as early as the following Thanksgiving.

# FAST CRAWFISH CURRY

LOBSTER BISQUE SOUP     1 13-ounce can
CONDENSED TOMATO SOUP     1 10¾-ounce can
CONDENSED CREAM OF MUSHROOM SOUP     1 10¾-ounce can
MILK     ½ cup
GREEN PEPPER     ¼ cup finely chopped
BUTTER     2 tablespoons, melted
CURRY POWDER     4 teaspoons
BLACK PEPPER     ⅛ teaspoon
RED PEPPER FLAKES     ¼ teaspoon
GARLIC SALT     ⅛ teaspoon
CRAWFISH MEAT     3 cups cooked and cleaned
DRY WHITE WINE     ½ cup
INSTANT RICE     ¾ cup

In large bowl combine first 5 ingredients. In small bowl combine next 5 ingredients. Add curry mixture to soup mixture. Fold in crawfish. Combine wine and rice; allow to stand 15 minutes; fold into soup-curry mixture. Pour into greased casserole. Cover and bake at 300° until bubbly (about 15 to 20 minutes). Serves 6.

.   .   .   .   .

In 1970 approximately twenty fishermen fished for crayfish in the Sacramento River delta from May 18 through September 10. They caught over 83,000 pounds at Courtland, California. The value of this catch totaled $32,430.

# CHICKEN AND CRAWFISH CASSEROLE

WHITE RICE    ¾ cup
CHICKEN LEGS    2
CHICKEN THIGHS    2
CHICKEN BREASTS    2, split
COOKING OIL    3 tablespoons
ONION    ½ cup chopped
GREEN PEPPER    ½ cup chopped
TOMATO SOUP    1 10¾-ounce can
HEAVY CREAM    1 cup
DRY SHERRY    ½ cup
SALT    1½ teaspoons
WORCESTERSHIRE SAUCE    ½ teaspoon
PEPPER    ¼ teaspoon
THYME    ¼ teaspoon
CRAWFISH MEAT    1 cup cooked and cleaned
PARSLEY    2 tablespoons chopped

Preheat oven to 350°. Cook rice as directed on package. Rinse chicken and pat dry. Heat Dutch oven. Add oil and brown chicken pieces; set aside. Sauté onion and green pepper until tender; then remove from heat. Into sautéed mixture stir soup, cream, sherry, salt, Worcestershire, pepper, and thyme; blend well. Add cooked rice, chicken, and crawfish. Bake in covered greased casserole for 60 minutes or until chicken is tender. Garnish with parsley. Makes 6 servings.

# CRAWFISH TETRAZZINI

BUTTER     2 tablespoons
FLOUR     2 tablespoons
SALT     ½ teaspoon
NUTMEG     dash
PEPPER     dash
CHICKEN BOUILLON or MILK     2 cups
SHERRY     1 tablespoon
SPAGHETTI     2 cups cooked
SLICED MUSHROOMS     1 4-ounce can, drained
CRAWFISH MEAT     2 or 3 cups cooked and cleaned
PARMESAN CHEESE     2 tablespoons grated
DRY BREAD CRUMBS     2 tablespoons
WATERCRESS or PARSLEY     to garnish

Melt butter. Blend in flour and seasonings. Add bouillon gradually. Cook until thick and smooth, stirring constantly. Add sherry. Mix half of this sauce with spaghetti and mushrooms; place in a well-greased casserole. Mix remainder of sauce with crawfish and place in center of spaghetti. Combine cheese and crumbs; sprinkle over top of crawfish mixture. Bake in moderate oven at 350° for 25 to 30 minutes. Garnish with watercress. Serves 6.

.     .     .     .     .

If, when catching crawfish, one catches you, don't shake or pull it off! Put your hand in the water and the crawdad will loosen its grip and swim away. You may have a bruise, but your skin will be intact.

# CRAWFISH PUFFS

BUTTER or MARGARINE     2 tablespoons
FLOUR     2 tablespoons
PAPRIKA     ¼ teaspoon
MILK     1 cup
EGG YOLKS     2, beaten
CRAWFISH MEAT     1½ cups cooked and cleaned
WHIPPING CREAM     1 cup
EGG WHITES     2, beaten

Melt butter. Blend in flour and paprika. Add milk gradually and cook until thick and smooth, stirring constantly; remove from heat. Add egg yolks and fold in crawfish. Whip cream and fold in beaten egg whites; blend cream mixture into crawfish mixture. Place in individual greased casseroles (6 or 8). Place casseroles in a pan of hot water and bake at 350° for 40 to 45 minutes or until firm in center. Makes 6 to 8 servings.

. . . . . .

The largest family of crawfish in North America, Cambaridae, has over 100 species and subspecies. Originating in the southeastern section of the United States, many species have spread north and eastward up the Mississippi River Valley and northward along the Atlantic Coast. Members of the family are found in many other places as well, such as Cuba, Guatemala, Honduras, and Mexico.

# CRAWDADS 'N' RICE

RICE    2 cups cooked
STUFFED OLIVES    ½ cup sliced
SMALL ONION    1, chopped
MEDIUM GREEN PEPPER    1, chopped
SHARP CHEESE    ½ cup grated
CRAWFISH MEAT    3 cups cooked and cleaned
FLOUR    4 tablespoons
MILK    2 cups
BUTTER    3 tablespoons, melted
SALT and PEPPER

Mix rice, olives, onion, green pepper, most of cheese, and crawfish together and put into a well-greased casserole. Combine flour, milk, and butter and season to taste; pour over ingredients in casserole. Sprinkle with remaining grated cheese. Bake at 350° for 30 minutes until top is nicely browned. Serves 6.

. . . . . .

Scientists believe that before the Ice Age, crawfish originated in some area of Europe or Asia and migrated to North America across the Bering Strait.

# CRAWFISH CHEESE BAKE

ONION      3 tablespoons chopped
BUTTER      3 tablespoons
FLOUR      ¼ cup
MILK or TOMATO JUICE      1½ cups
SALT      ½ teaspoon
DRY MUSTARD      ¼ teaspoon
PEPPER      dash
CHEDDAR CHEESE      1 cup grated
CRAWFISH MEAT      1 cup cooked and cleaned
BUTTER      1 tablespoon, melted
DRY BREAD CRUMBS      ¼ cup

Sauté onion in butter until tender. Blend in flour, milk, and seasonings. Cook until thick, stirring constantly. Add ¾ cup cheese and heat until melted. Add crawfish and stir well. Pour into 6 well-greased individual casseroles. Combine butter, bread crumbs, and remaining cheese. Sprinkle on top of casseroles. Bake in hot oven (400°) for 10 minutes or until brown on top. Serves 6.

. . . . . .

The crawfish genus *Pacifastacus* includes virtually all the crawfish species found from the Pacific Coast eastward to the Rocky Mountains and from Alaska south to Mexico. These are sometimes called European crayfish because they were commonly found in Europe as well as in Asia.

# CRAWFISH FONDUE

DAY-OLD WHITE BREAD   8 slices, buttered
CRAWFISH MEAT   3 cups cooked and cleaned
GREEN PEPPER   ¼ cup chopped
PARMESAN CHEESE   1 cup grated
EGGS   3
DRY MUSTARD   ¼ teaspoon
SALT   ½ teaspoon
PEPPER   dash
MILK   2 cups
PAPRIKA

Remove crusts from bread and cube into ½-inch pieces. Place half of bread cubes into a well-greased baking dish and cover with crawfish, green pepper, and half of cheese. Top with remaining bread cubes. Combine eggs, mustard, salt, and pepper; beat until frothy; add milk and mix well. Pour over crawfish mixture. Sprinkle with paprika. Bake in moderate oven (350°) for about 1 hour or until firm in center. Remove from oven and allow to stand 5 minutes before serving. Serves 6.

. . . . . .

In Louisiana, the crayfish season has peaked by May, and by June the harvest generally tapers off. By this time crayfish flesh has become tough.

# CRAWFISH AND ARTICHOKES

MUSHROOMS　　1 pound, sliced
BUTTER　　7 tablespoons
FROZEN ARTICHOKE HEARTS　　1 9-ounce package, cooked
CRAWFISH MEAT　　4 cups cooked and cleaned
FLOUR　　3 tablespoons
MILK　　2 cups
SALT　　⅛ teaspoon
PEPPER　　dash
DRY SHERRY　　¼ cup
WORCESTERSHIRE SAUCE　　1 tablespoon
PARMESAN CHEESE　　½ cup grated

Sauté mushrooms in 4 tablespoons butter until tender. Place artichokes, crawfish, and mushrooms in a greased casserole. Combine remaining 3 tablespoons butter, flour, milk, salt, and pepper in pan, stirring constantly. Cook until bubbly and creamy; remove from heat. Stir in sherry and Worcestershire sauce and pour over mixture in casserole. Sprinkle cheese on top. Bake at 375° for 20 minutes. Serves 8 to 10.

. . . . . .

The Houma Indians, a fierce and respected tribe who once roamed what is now Terrebonne Parish, Louisiana, held the crawfish in such high regard that they used it as a battle symbol.

# CRAWFISH DE JONGHE

| | |
|---:|:---|
| DRY BREAD CRUMBS | 3 cups |
| BUTTER | 1¼ cups |
| GREEN ONION | ½ cup chopped |
| GREEN PEPPER | ½ cup chopped |
| GARLIC CLOVES | 3, finely chopped |
| PARSLEY | 1½ tablespoons chopped |
| DRIED CHERVIL | ½ teaspoon |
| POWDERED TARRAGON | 1 to 2 tablespoons (to taste) |
| NUTMEG | ½ teaspoon |
| THYME | ½ teaspoon |
| MACE | dash |
| SHERRY | 1 cup |
| CRAWFISH MEAT | 4 cups cooked and cleaned |

Combine 2 cups crumbs, 1 cup butter, green onion, green pepper, garlic, parsley, chervil, tarragon, nutmeg, thyme, mace, and sherry. Place alternate layers of crawfish and crumb mixture in a well-greased casserole. Combine ¼ cup butter and 1 cup crumbs to form topping; sprinkle over top of casserole. Bake in moderate oven at 350° for 1 hour until well browned. Serves 6.

. . . . . .

Although crawfish may be caught in almost any body of fresh water in North America, they are found in greatest abundance in Louisiana, Mississippi, Texas, Alabama, and Oregon.

# WEIRD AND WONDERFUL CASSEROLE

SMALL EGGPLANT    1
VEGETABLE OIL      for frying
CHICKEN BOUILLON CUBE      1
WATER    2½ cups hot*
SALAD OIL    4 tablespoons
BUTTER    1 tablespoon
RICE    1 cup
SALT    1 teaspoon
BAY LEAF    1
GARLIC CLOVES    2, finely chopped
MEDIUM ONIONS    2, finely chopped
GREEN PEPPERS    2, finely chopped
LARGE TOMATOES    4, peeled
STUFFED OLIVES    ½ cup sliced
PAPRIKA    2 tablespoons
CAYENNE    ⅛ teaspoon
SMALL CLAMS    1 cup (or 1 6½-ounce can) chopped
CRAWFISH MEAT    2 cups cooked and cleaned
CHEDDAR CHEESE    1½ cups, grated

Cube ½-inch slices of eggplant and fry in oil. Set aside for casserole. Dissolve bouillon cube in water. Heat salad oil and butter in 3-quart saucepan, add rice, and stir to coat rice. Add bouillon, salt, and bay leaf and bring to a boil. Lower heat and simmer covered without stirring for 25 minutes. Preheat oven to 375°. In a heavy skillet or Dutch oven, sauté garlic, onion, and green pepper until tender. Chop 2 tomatoes and add to sautéed vegetables. Add olives, paprika, and cayenne. Cook 5 minutes. Set aside. Add clams, crawfish, and rice mixture to tomato mixture. Stir gently to mix. Put into 4-quart casserole that has been generously greased. Slice remaining 2 tomatoes and arrange alternately around edge of casserole with fried eggplant. Sprinkle cheese over all. Bake 15 minutes or until cheese is bubbly. Serves 8.

*Or use broth from canned clams as part of liquid.

# SCAPPOOSE CRAWFISH AND CRAB SPECIAL

WILD and WHITE RICE MIX    2 6-ounce packages
CRAB MEAT    2 6½-ounce cans
CRAWFISH MEAT    3 cups cooked and cleaned
CONDENSED MUSHROOM SOUP    3 10¾-ounce cans
GREEN PEPPER    ⅓ cup finely chopped
CELERY    1 cup finely chopped
PIMIENTO    1 2-ounce jar, drained and chopped
LEMON JUICE    2 tablespoons
PARSLEY    to garnish
RIPE OLIVES    to garnish

Cook rice as directed on packages. Drain crab meat and remove cartilage. Preheat oven to 325°. Grease 4-quart casserole. Combine all ingredients except parsley and olives in casserole and mix thoroughly. Bake 1 hour uncovered. Garnish with parsley and olives. Serves 10 to 12.

. . . . . .

When a cluster of eggs appears on the underside of a female red swamp crayfish's tail, she is said to be "in berry." The eggs hatch in two to three weeks and the young remain attached to the female for a week or two as they grow and molt twice. After these molts the strongest survivors are ready to fend for themselves and will leave the burrow which has been their nursery and home.

# RIVER HOUSE SUPPER

POTATOES    4 cups cooked and thinly sliced
CRAWFISH MEAT    1½ pounds cooked and cleaned (about 3 cups)
BACON    6 slices, diced small
CELERY    1 cup sliced
ONION    1 cup chopped
GREEN PEPPER    1 cup cut into strips
FLOUR    2 tablespoons
SALT    1½ teaspoons
SUGAR    3 tablespoons
CELERY SEED    ½ teaspoon
PAPRIKA    ½ teaspoon
WATER    1 cup
VINEGAR    ½ cup
PIMIENTO    ¼ cup chopped
PARSLEY    ¼ cup chopped

Put potatoes into well-greased casserole. Put crawfish on top of potatoes. Cook bacon until crisp, remove to paper towel to drain, and hold in reserve. Cook celery, onion, and green pepper in bacon fat until tender. Stir in flour and next 4 ingredients. Add water and vinegar, slowly stirring mixture until thick. Add pimiento and bacon pieces. Spoon mixture over potatoes and crawfish. Bake at 300° until casserole is bubbly and browned. Garnish with parsley. Serves 6.

EGG NOODLES      1 6- to 8-ounce package of ¼-inch noodles
          ONION      ¼, finely chopped
    GREEN PEPPER      ¼, finely chopped
      MUSHROOMS      1 4-ounce can, drained
          BUTTER      1 tablespoon
  CRAWFISH MEAT      2 cups cooked and cleaned
  MEDIUM TOMATO      1, chopped and drained
      LEMON JUICE      1 tablespoon
            SALT      ¼ teaspoon
          PEPPER      ⅛ teaspoon
      MAYONNAISE      ¾ cup
          CHEESE      ½ cup shredded

Cook noodles according to package directions. Sauté onion, green pepper, and mushrooms in butter until tender. Stir together with next 6
ingredients. Add noodles and mix well. Place in buttered 2-quart casserole. Top with cheese. Bake at 400° for 20 minutes or until cheese
melts. Serves 6.

.   .   .   .   .   .

Among the crayfish's numerous appendages are six pairs used principally
for handling and mincing food.

# CRAWFISH SORRENTO

MUSHROOM SOUP     2 10¾-ounce cans
MILK     1 cup
PARMESAN CHEESE     1 cup grated
ELBOW MACARONI     2 cups, cooked and drained
CRAWFISH MEAT     2 cups cooked and cleaned
SLICED MUSHROOMS     1 4-ounce can
PIMIENTO     ¼ cup chopped
PEPPER     ⅛ teaspoon
GARLIC SALT     1 teaspoon
BUTTER     2 teaspoons

Mix soup and milk. Heat until it bubbles. Add ½ cup cheese. Pour into greased casserole. Mix in rest of ingredients except remaining cheese and butter. Sprinkle remaining cheese on top. Dot with butter. Bake at 350° until brown (30 to 45 minutes). Serves 8 to 10.

.   .   .   .   .   .

In 1890 the American crayfish, called *Orconectes limosus* by marine biologists, was taken to Poland by Max von den Borne. He released them in a pond. Because of their resistance to a disease that had almost wiped out the European crayfish, their migratory habits, and human assistance, these transplants spread throughout the country. The American crayfish now ranks third in the Polish shellfish industry. However, the Poles changed the name to striped crayfish.

# CRAWFISH MUSHROOM CASSEROLE

| | |
|---|---|
| BUTTER | 2½ tablespoons |
| FLOUR | 2½ tablespoons |
| CHEDDAR CHEESE | 4 tablespoons shredded |
| MILK | ½ cup |
| SLICED MUSHROOMS | 1 4-ounce can, drained |
| CRAWFISH MEAT | 1 cup cooked and cleaned |
| PIMIENTO | 1, thinly sliced |
| BREAD CRUMBS | |
| BUTTER | as needed |
| CHEESE | cubed |
| PAPRIKA | |

Blend first 3 ingredients in top of double boiler. Add milk. Cook until thickened. Add mushrooms, crawfish, and most of pimiento. Pour into buttered casserole. Sprinkle with bread crumbs, dot with butter and cheese cubes, sprinkle with paprika, and garnish with pimiento strips. Bake at 350° until bubbly. Serve with rice or noodles. Serves 4 to 6.

# COMPANY CRAWFISH

ARTICHOKE HEARTS     1 14-ounce can, drained
CRAWFISH MEAT     1½ cups cooked and cleaned
SLICED MUSHROOMS     1 4-ounce can, drained
BUTTER or MARGARINE     2 tablespoons
FLOUR     2 tablespoons
CAYENNE     dash
HALF-AND-HALF or EVAPORATED MILK     1 cup
SHERRY     2 tablespoons
PARMESAN CHEESE     1 tablespoon grated
CEREAL CRUMBS     2 tablespoons
PAPRIKA

Cut artichokes in half and place in well-greased, shallow casserole. Cover with crawfish and mushrooms. In saucepan, melt butter. Blend in flour and cayenne. Add half-and-half gradually. Cook until thick, stirring constantly. Stir in sherry. Pour sauce over crawfish and mushrooms. Blend cheese and crumbs; sprinkle over top. Sprinkle with paprika. Bake in very hot oven (450°) for 12 to 14 minutes. Serves 6.

# TOMATO-CRAWFISH BAKE

BUTTER    1 tablespoon
SOFT BREAD CRUMBS    ½ cup
THIN SPAGHETTI    2½ cups small pieces, cooked and drained
CONDENSED TOMATO SOUP    1 10¾-ounce can
EVAPORATED MILK    1 13-ounce can
CRAWFISH MEAT    1 cup cooked and cleaned
CHEESE    1 cup grated
GREEN PEPPER    ¼ tablespoon minced
SALT    ½ teaspoon
THYME    dash

Melt butter in a small pan; toss bread crumbs in butter; set aside. Combine all ingredients except buttered crumbs in casserole. Top with crumbs. Bake at 400° until top browns (30 minutes). Serves 6.

# CRAWFISH HARPIN CASSEROLE

| | |
|---|---|
| CRAWFISH MEAT | 2 cups cooked and cleaned |
| LEMON JUICE | 1 tablespoon |
| SALAD OIL | 3 tablespoons |
| RICE | ¾ cup |
| GREEN PEPPER | ¼ cup minced |
| ONION | ¼ cup minced |
| BUTTER | 2 tablespoons |
| SALT | 1 teaspoon |
| PEPPER | ⅛ teaspoon |
| MACE | ⅛ teaspoon |
| CAYENNE | dash |
| TOMATO SOUP | 1 10¾-ounce can |
| HEAVY CREAM | 1 cup |
| SHERRY | ½ cup |
| SLIVERED ALMONDS | ½ cup |
| PAPRIKA | |

Place crawfish meat in 2-quart casserole. Sprinkle with lemon juice and oil. Cook rice as directed on package. Combine crawfish and rice and chill. About 70 minutes before serving, preheat oven to 350°. Sauté green pepper and onion in butter for 5 minutes and add to rice mixture. Add seasonings, soup, cream, and sherry; mix. Top with almonds and paprika. Bake at 350° until browned and bubbly (about 1 hour). Serves 6 to 8.

# QUICK CRAWFISH CURRY CASSEROLE

FROZEN CHINESE PEA PODS    1 6-ounce package or
(FRESH CHINESE PEA PODS    2 cups cooked)
CURRY SAUCE MIX    1¼-ounce package
MAYONNAISE    ½ cup
CRAWFISH MEAT    2 cups cooked and cleaned
WATER CHESTNUTS    1 8-ounce can, drained and sliced
BLANCHED WHOLE ALMONDS    1 4½-ounce can
BUTTER    1 tablespoon
WHITE RICE    6 servings, cooked and hot
PREPARED CHUTNEY

Cook pea pods as directed on package. Preheat oven to 375°. Make curry sauce as directed on package; blend in mayonnaise. Combine crawfish, pea pods, water chestnuts, and curry sauce in 1½-quart casserole. Bake uncovered for 20 minutes. Sauté almonds in butter; sprinkle over top of casserole. Serve with rice and chutney. Makes 6 servings.

# Entrées

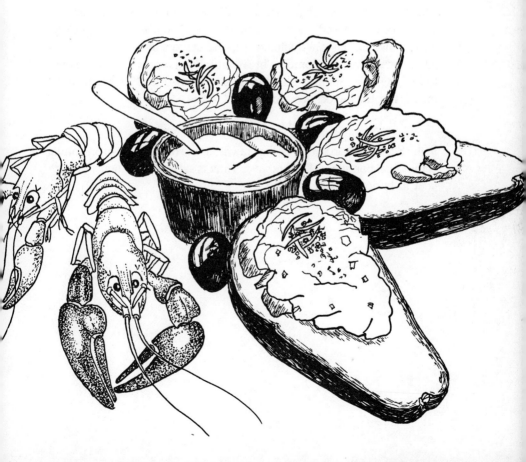

# CRAWFISH AVOCADO

LARGE AVOCADOS 3
LEMON JUICE
SALT ½ teaspoon
CRAWFISH MEAT 2 cups cooked and cleaned
CELERY ⅓ cup chopped
EGGS 3, hard-cooked and chopped
PIMIENTO 3 tablespoons chopped
ONION 1 tablespoon chopped
MAYONNAISE ½ cup
FINE BREAD CRUMBS 3 tablespoons
BUTTER 1 tablespoon, melted
SLIVERED ALMONDS 2 tablespoons

Cut avocados in half lengthwise. Sprinkle with lemon juice and some of salt. Place on greased platter or baking pan. Combine crawfish, celery, eggs, pimiento, onion, remaining salt, and mayonnaise. Spoon mixture into avocado halves. Combine bread crumbs with butter. Sprinkle over top of mixture. Sprinkle almonds over all. Bake at 350° for 5 to 10 minutes or until avocados are tender. Serves 6.

. . . . . .

In the Scandinavian countries the crawfish is the main object of an annual ceremonial banquet called *krebfest*. Time is set aside in August of each year to honor and eat crawfish.

# CRAWFISH IN LEMON BUTTER

CRAWFISH MEAT      3 cups cooked and cleaned
BUTTER or MARGARINE      ¼ cup
LEMON JUICE      1 tablespoon
SALT      ¼ teaspoon
PEPPER      dash
CAPERS      2 tablespoons

Sauté crawfish gently in butter, stirring frequently. Cook until lightly browned. Remove and place on platter. To browned butter, add lemon juice and seasonings. Pour over crawfish and garnish with capers. Serve with baked rice. Serves 6.

. . . . . .

Only the most skilled and highly trained scientific eye can identify the species of crawfish. According to *McClane's New Standard Fishing Encyclopedia,* ". . . the pleopod found on the male is by far the most useful [way to identify the species]. It is the modified first swimmeret which becomes hardened and assumes a distinctive shape, and is used to clasp the female during mating." However, even determining the sex of the crawfish is nearly impossible for most of us. After checking hundreds and hundreds of the critters, this writer is inclined to believe that only another crawfish knows for sure!

# CRAWFISH IN SOUR CREAM

SLICED MUSHROOMS     1 4-ounce can, drained
GREEN ONION     2 tablespoons chopped
BUTTER     2 tablespoons, melted
FLOUR     1 tablespoon
CREAM OF SHRIMP SOUP     1 10¾-ounce can
SOUR CREAM     1 cup
PEPPER     dash
CRAWFISH MEAT     1 cup cooked and cleaned
TOAST POINTS or SAFFRON RICE
PARSLEY     to garnish

Sauté mushrooms and green onion in butter until tender. Blend in flour. Add soup. Cook until thick, stirring constantly. Add sour cream, pepper, and crawfish. Heat. Serve on toast points. Garnish with parsley. Serves 6.

.   .   .   .   .   .

Crawfish prefer clean water in which to live. In the Gulf States they thrive at temperatures between fifty-three and sixty-six degrees, about ten degrees less in the Northwest. It is important for anyone catching crawfish for table food to be absolutely certain that the water in which they are caught is up to national and state health standards. Your local fish and game commissioner can tell you if the water is safe.

# DEEP-FRIED CRAWFISH

### BATTER:
FLOUR    ½ cup
BAKING POWDER    ¼ teaspoon
SUGAR    1 teaspoon
SALT    1 teaspoon
EGG    1, beaten
MILK    ½ cup

CRAWFISH MEAT    2 cups cooked and cleaned
COOKING OIL

Make batter by combining dry ingredients, egg, and milk. Dip each crawfish bit into batter and fry immediately in deep fat over medium heat (375°) until a golden brown. Drain on absorbent paper and serve with cocktail sauce (see index).

Variations in Batter: Instead of using milk as liquid, substitute beer or lemonade. Pancake or biscuit mix may replace other dry ingredients in batter.

. . . . . .

The life-span of most species of crawfish east of the Rocky Mountains ranges from one to three years. Some of the western United States and European species reach the ripe old age of six or seven years.

# TOMATOES STUFFED WITH CRAWFISH

LARGE TOMATOES    6
SALT    2 teaspoons
CHEESE    ½ cup grated
RICE    1 cup cooked
EGG    1, beaten
PEPPER    dash
CRAWFISH MEAT    3 cups cooked and cleaned
BUTTER or OIL    1 tablespoon, melted
DRY BREAD CRUMBS    ¼ cup

Wash tomatoes. Remove stem ends and centers. Sprinkle with 1 teaspoon salt. Combine cheese, rice, egg, rest of seasoning, and crawfish; fill tomatoes with mixture. Combine butter and crumbs and sprinkle over tops of tomatoes. Place in well-greased baking pan. Bake in moderate oven (350°) for 30 to 40 minutes, or until tomatoes are tender. Serves 6.

. . . . . .

Life for Louisiana's red swamp crawfish begins in a hole in the ground called a burrow. These burrows may be only a few inches deep, when a temporary home, or they can be as deep as forty inches. Most crawfish burrows have a mud chimney which is capped with a mud plug.

# CRAWFISH IN PATTY SHELLS

SLICED MUSHROOMS    1 4-ounce can, drained
GREEN PEPPER    2 tablespoons chopped
BUTTER    3 tablespoons
FLOUR    3 tablespoons
CAYENNE    dash
MILK    1½ cups
PIMIENTO    2 tablespoons chopped
CRAWFISH MEAT    3 cups cooked and cleaned
PATTY SHELLS    6, baked

Cook mushrooms and green pepper in butter until tender. Blend in flour and cayenne. Add milk gradually. Cook until thick, stirring constantly. Add pimiento. Add crawfish. Heat thoroughly. Serve in patty shells. Serves 6.

.   .   .   .   .   .

Cities Service Oil Company has become interested in crayfish farming in the Cajun country of Louisiana and is making crayfish available to many places that are serviced by commercial airlines. Now Louisiana crayfish can be purchased nationwide.

# CRAWFISH WIGGLE

BUTTER ¼ cup
FLOUR ½ cup
SALT 1 teaspoon
MILK 2 cups
PEAS 1 cup, cooked
CRAWFISH MEAT 1 cup cooked and cleaned
PATTY SHELLS, TOAST POINTS, or RICE
EGGS hard-cooked and sliced
PARSLEY to garnish

Melt butter. Blend in flour and salt. Add milk gradually and cook, stirring constantly until mixture is smooth and thick. Gently stir in peas and crawfish. Heat and serve in patty shells. Garnish with eggs and parsley. Serves 4 to 6.

．　．　．　．　．

Mating for most crawfish in the southern states occurs in May. At mating time the female digs a burrow which the male enters later. At that time the male deposits sperm in an external cuplike receptacle on the female. The female then carries the sperm until she lays eggs later in the summer or in the early fall. As the eggs are laid, they are fertilized by the sperm held by the female. After this fertilization process, the eggs are attached to the swimmerets on the female's tail by a sticky substance, which is called glair. The number of eggs a female lays varies from species to species. She may lay as few as a dozen or as many as 700.

# FRIED CRAWFISH CAKES

ONION     2 tablespoons chopped
BUTTER or MARGARINE     2 tablespoons
CRAWFISH MEAT     1½ cups cooked and cleaned
EGG     1, beaten
SALT     ½ teaspoon
PEPPER     dash
CAYENNE     dash
FINE, DRY BREAD CRUMBS     ½ cup
VEGETABLE OIL
PARSLEY     2 tablespoons chopped
LEMON WEDGES

Sauté onion in butter until tender. Combine crawfish, egg, salt, pepper, and cayenne. Shape into 6 patties and roll in bread crumbs. Heat heavy skillet into which vegetable oil has been poured to a depth of ⅛ inch. Heat to hot but not smoking. Fry cakes at moderate heat. When brown on 1 side, turn carefully and fry other side to brown. Drain on absorbent paper. Garnish with parsley and lemon wedges. For a variation, shape crawfish mixture into walnut-sized balls, fry, and serve as appetizers. Makes 6 patties or 18 balls.

.     .     .     .     .

The rarest of the North American crawfish is called *Cambarellus*. It probably originated in northern Mexico and spread northeast through the southern United States. All members of this crawfish genus are small and are called dwarf crayfish.

# CURRIED CRAWFISH

ONION     ½ cup chopped
BUTTER     6 tablespoons
FLOUR     6 tablespoons
SALT     2 teaspoons
CURRY POWDER     2 teaspoons
POWDERED GINGER     ½ teaspoon
MILK     4 cups
CRAWFISH MEAT     4 cups cooked and cleaned
RICE     cooked
CONDIMENTS:
ONION     chopped
GREEN PEPPER     chopped
CHOPPED NUTS
GRATED COCONUT
CHUTNEY

Fry onion in butter until tender. Blend in flour and seasonings. Add milk gradually. Cook until thick, stirring constantly. Add crawfish to heat. Serve curry dish with rice. Place condiments in small bowls for individual use. Serves 6.

.   .   .   .   .

In Louisiana crawfish are honored at festivals and jubilees. Crawfish races and contests are held to find the biggest or fastest crawfish in some areas. These festivities are usually followed by "crawfish feeds," which are enjoyed by all.

# CRAWFISH NEWBURG

BUTTER or MARGARINE    ⅓ cup
FLOUR    3 tablespoons
SALT    ½ teaspoon
PAPRIKA    ½ teaspoon
CAYENNE    dash
COFFEE CREAM    1½ cups
EGG YOLKS    3, beaten
CRAWFISH MEAT    1½ cups cooked and cleaned
SHERRY    2 tablespoons
TOAST POINTS

Melt butter; blend in flour and seasonings. Add cream gradually and cook over low heat until thick and smooth, stirring constantly. Add egg yolks. Add crawfish. Heat but do not boil. Remove from heat and slowly stir in sherry. Serve immediately on toast points. My family enjoys crumbling blue cheese on top of Newburg. Serves 6.

. . . . . .

The crayfish genus *Orconectes* has over sixty species and subspecies. This genus is found primarily in the Mississippi and Great Lakes drainage systems. Its members have spread west to the Rocky Mountains, north into Canada, and south to the Gulf of Mexico.

# EASY CRAWFISH THERMIDOR

SLICED MUSHROOMS     1 4-ounce can, drained
BUTTER     1 tablespoon, melted
CREAM OF SHRIMP SOUP     2 13-ounce cans
CRAWFISH MEAT     3 cups cooked and cleaned
MILK     ½ cup
PAPRIKA     ¼ teaspoon
SHERRY     3 tablespoons

Mix all ingredients in top of double boiler and stir occasionally until thoroughly heated. Or, mix all ingredients thoroughly, pour into individual casseroles, and broil until brown. Serves 6.

# CRAWFISH BOATS

CRAWFISH MEAT      2 cups cooked and cleaned
RIPE OLIVES      1 cup chopped
SOFT BREAD CRUMBS      1½ cups
GARLIC CLOVES      2, crushed
PARSLEY      3 tablespoons chopped
GREEN PEPPER      1, finely chopped
EGGS      2, lightly beaten
MEDIUM ZUCCHINIS      6, each cut in half lengthwise
VEGETABLE OIL and WHITE WINE      in equal parts


Crumble crawfish meat in a bowl. Add olives, bread crumbs, garlic, parsley, green pepper, and eggs. Steam or boil zucchini halves for 5 minutes. Scoop out seeds, leaving shell of ¼-inch thickness. Mound crawfish stuffing in zucchini. Place on greased cookie sheet or in greased shallow pan. Bake at 350° for about 30 minutes, basting occasionally with oil and wine mix. Serves 6.


·   ·   ·   ·   ·


In southern Louisiana most crawfish caught for food are red swamp crawfish (*Procambarus clarkii*). Further north in Louisiana the white river crawfish (*Procambarus blandingi*) is also used for food. There is no bag limit or closed season for crawfish in Louisiana, but it has been found that they are most easily caught when the water temperature is between fifty-five and sixty-six degrees. When water temperature is cold, the crawfish become sluggish.

# OVEN-FRIED CRAWFISH

CRAWFISH MEAT     2 cups cooked and cleaned
BUTTER     6 tablespoons, melted
ROQUEFORT DRESSING     1-pint jar
SEASONED BREAD CUBES     1 cup

Grease shallow baking pan generously. Spread crawfish meat over bottom of pan. Pour melted butter over it. Cover with Roquefort dressing. Top with seasoned cubes. Bake 20 minutes at 350°. Serves 4.

.   .   .   .   .   .

Some species of crayfish are used as biological control agents in keeping down the growth of aquatic weeds in trout lakes.

CRAWFISH MEAT      1½ cups cooked and cleaned
CHEDDAR CHEESE SOUP      1 11-ounce can
SMALL ONION      1, finely minced
RIPE OLIVES      9, sliced into circles
WORCESTERSHIRE SAUCE      ¼ teaspoon
TABASCO SAUCE      5 drops
TOAST POINTS, ENGLISH MUFFINS, or RICE
PAPRIKA      to garnish
PARSLEY      to garnish
EGGS      hard-cooked and sliced, to garnish

Mix first 6 ingredients together and serve on toast points. Garnish with paprika, parsley, and eggs. Serves 4.

.    .    .    .    .    .

To catch crawfish by the can or bucket method, place bait in a large can or bucket and weight it to prevent its floating downstream. Crawfish will crawl into the bucket or can and eat your offering. Quickly bring the container to the surface and pour your catch into a keeping receptacle.

# CRAWFISH STUFFED PEPPERS

BUTTER     6 tablespoons
CRAWFISH FAT     ¼ cup
ONION     1½ cups minced
CELERY     1 cup minced
CRAWFISH TAILS     1 pound cooked and cleaned or
(CRAWFISH MEAT     1 cup cooked and cleaned)
SOFT BREAD CRUMBS     1½ cups
GREEN ONIONS     ¼ cup minced
PARSLEY     ¼ cup minced
GREEN PEPPERS     8 to 10
DRY BREAD CRUMBS     approximately 3 cups, for coating
SALT     1¼ teaspoons
CRUSHED RED PEPPER     ¼ teaspoon
BLACK PEPPER     ¼ teaspoon
EGGS     2, slightly beaten
VEGETABLE OIL     enough to deep fry

Heat butter and crawfish fat. Add onion and celery. Cook until soft. Add crawfish. Simmer 15 minutes. Remove from heat and add soft bread crumbs, green onions, and parsley. Cut green peppers in fourths or sixths, depending on size. Add stuffing, packing well. Season dry bread crumbs with salt, red and black pepper. Dip stuffed peppers into egg and coat with bread crumbs. Fry in deep fat at 375° 2 to 3 minutes until golden brown. Drain on paper towels. Or, instead of frying, bake at 400° until golden brown. These can be frozen and used later. Serves 8 to 10.

# International
# and
# Southern Entrées
# and Deep South
# Specials

# CRAWFISH FRICASSEE

LIVE CRAWFISH     10 pounds
FLOUR     1 tablespoon
BUTTER     1 tablespoon
ONION     2 tablespoons chopped
WATER     as needed
RICE, TOAST, or WHITE POTATOES     as desired

Drop crawfish into boiling water and cook until red; shell and devein. Brown flour in butter. Add onion. Add crawfish and enough water to make a gravy. Serve over rice. Serves 6 to 8.

.  .  .  .  .  .

For the most part, crawfish are burrowers. Some species live their entire lives underground. However, there are some that never burrow.

# CREAMY HERBAL CRAWFISH

LIVE CRAWFISH      about 2 pounds (2 cups cooked meat)
BOILING RECIPE II      see index
BUTTER      3 tablespoons
FLOUR      3 tablespoons
PEPPER      to taste
EVAPORATED MILK or LIGHT CREAM      1 cup
PARMESAN CHEESE      1 tablespoon grated
PARSLEY      1 teaspoon finely chopped
CHIVES      1 teaspoon finely chopped
BASIL LEAVES      ½ teaspoon
TARRAGON LEAVES      ¼ teaspoon
DRY WHITE WINE      ⅓ cup
RICE or NOODLES      as desired
PARSLEY SPRIGS      to garnish
PAPRIKA      sprinkle

Boil crawfish as described in boiling recipe II (with pickling spice); shell and devein; set aside. Save 1 cup crawfish broth. Melt butter; blend in flour and pepper; cook until bubbly. Gradually add milk, broth, and cheese. Heat, stirring until sauce thickens. Add parsley, chives, basil, tarragon, wine, and crawfish and cook over *low* heat, stirring until crawfish is thoroughly heated. Serve over rice. Garnish with parsley. Sprinkle with paprika. Serves 6 to 8.

# CRAWFISH ITALIENNE

GARLIC CLOVES    2, minced
OLIVE OIL    4 tablespoons
CRAWFISH MEAT    3 cups cooked and cleaned
WATER    as needed
SALT    ½ teaspoon
PEPPER    to taste
SPAGHETTI    1½ pounds, cooked
PARMESAN CHEESE    grated, to garnish
PARSLEY    5 tablespoons minced

Cook garlic in olive oil until tender. Add crawfish. Heat slowly, adding small amounts of water as needed to keep mixture moist until thoroughly heated. Sprinkle with salt and pepper. Spoon over spaghetti. Garnish with Parmesan cheese and parsley. Serves 6.

.    .    .    .    .

There is a species of crawfish found in the eastern and midwestern states that reaches five to six inches in length. It is edible and can be found in ponds, brooks, rivers, and lakes from the Great Lakes to the Atlantic Coast. The scientific name is *Procambarus acutus,* but it is generally called crawfish, crayfish, or crawdad.

# CHINESE CRAWFISH DINNER

GARLIC    3 or 4 thin slices
PEANUT OIL    ¼ cup
LARGE ONIONS    2, sliced
CELERY    2 cups sliced
MUSHROOMS    2 cups sliced
SOYBEANS    2 cups cooked
BAMBOO SHOOTS    1 8½-ounce can, drained and sliced
BEAN SPROUTS    1 8-ounce can, drained
WATER CHESTNUTS    1 8-ounce can, drained and sliced
WATER    1 cup
CHICKEN BOUILLON    2 tablespoons
SOY SAUCE    3 tablespoons
FRESH SPINACH    3 cups finely shredded
CORNSTARCH    2 tablespoons
COLD WATER    2 tablespoons
CRAWFISH MEAT    2 or 3 cups cooked and cleaned
WHITE or BROWN RICE    3 cups cooked

Brown garlic in oil and remove from skillet. Sauté onions until soft; stir in celery and cook 2 minutes. Stir in mushrooms and cook another 2 minutes. Mash soybeans. Add soybeans, bamboo shoots, bean sprouts, and water chestnuts to skillet. Mix 1 cup water with bouillon and soy sauce; add to skillet. Bring mixture to a boil. Lower heat to simmer and cook 5 minutes. Add spinach. Cover and simmer 2 minutes. Mix cornstarch and 2 tablespoons cold water in a cup. Add to skillet, stirring constantly until mixture thickens and is clear. Add crawfish; heat to simmer. Serve on rice. Serves 6.

# CRAWFISH TACOS I

TACO SHELLS     12
CRAWFISH MEAT     3 cups cooked and cleaned
LETTUCE     2 cups shredded
MEDIUM TOMATO     1, finely chopped and drained
SMALL ONION     1, finely chopped
SHARP CHEESE     ½ cup shredded
TACO SAUCE or FAVORITE COCKTAIL SAUCE

Preheat oven to 250°; bake taco shells 10 minutes. Remove from oven. Place crawfish in bottom of shells. Fill remainder of shell with lettuce, tomato, and onion. Top with cheese. Sprinkle with sauce. Makes 12 tacos.

.   .   .   .   .

Crawfish can be seen in varying hues of red, green, brown, and black. Those living in deep caves in the South have been found white, totally without pigment.

# CRAWDAD TACOS II

CRAWFISH MEAT    2 cups cooked and cleaned
MAYONNAISE    ½ cup
ONION    ¼ cup chopped
TACO SHELLS    12
CHEESE    2 cups coarsely shredded
LETTUCE    2 cups finely chopped
TOMATOES    2 cups chopped, drained
TABASCO SAUCE or HOT SAUCE    4 or 5 shakes

Combine first 3 ingredients. Set aside. Place taco shells in 9×13×2-inch pan. Sprinkle most of cheese generously over shells so that when placed in a 300° oven, the fold will be covered with melted cheese. When cheese melts, remove from oven. Place about 2 tablespoons crawfish mixture on top of cheese. Sprinkle with lettuce and then with tomato. Scatter remaining cheese sparingly on top. Sprinkle with Tabasco. Serves 6.

.    .    .    .    .    .

There are nineteen segments in the adult body of a crawfish. The first five segments form the head, the next eight form the thorax, and the last six form the tail or abdomen.

# SWEET AND SOUR CRAWFISH

FLOUR   ¼ cup
SALT   1 teaspoon
CRAWFISH MEAT   3 cups cooked and cleaned
VEGETABLE or PEANUT OIL   enough for frying
CIDER VINEGAR   ½ cup
SUGAR   1 cup
WATER   1⅓ cups
CHICKEN BOUILLON CUBES   3
LARGE GREEN PEPPER   1, cut into ¼-inch rings
PINEAPPLE CHUNKS   1 cup drained
WATER   1½ tablespoons
CORNSTARCH   3 tablespoons
SOY SAUCE   1½ teaspoons
RICE   1½ cups, cooked

Sprinkle flour and salt over crawfish. Brown crawfish lightly in oil; remove from frying pan. In pan combine vinegar, sugar, 1⅓ cups water, bouillon cubes, green pepper, and pineapple; cook slowly for 10 minutes. Combine remaining water, cornstarch, and soy sauce in a cup; gradually add it to hot sauce, stirring constantly. Cook until thick. Pour over crawfish and serve with rice. Serves 6.

. . . . . .

Crawfish are nocturnal in habit. They are secretive and shy and remain hidden under rocks and logs unless tempted out of their hiding places by food.

# CRAWFISH PIZZA

ONION   ⅓ cup chopped
GARLIC CLOVES   3, finely chopped
BUTTER   as needed
ITALIAN-STYLE TOMATO PASTE   3 6-ounce cans
PARSLEY   ⅓ cup chopped
OREGANO   1½ teaspoons
UNBAKED PIZZA CRUSTS   3  9-inch crusts
VEGETABLE OIL   as needed
CRAWFISH MEAT   3 cups cooked and cleaned
MOZZARELLA CHEESE   ¾ pound, thinly sliced
RIPE OLIVES   ½ cup thinly sliced
PARMESAN CHEESE   ½ cup grated

Cook onion and garlic in butter until tender. Add tomato paste; simmer for 5 minutes. Remove from heat. Add parsley and oregano. Place pizza crusts on well-greased cookie sheets. Brush with vegetable oil. Cover each crust with ⅓ of sauce, ⅓ of crawfish, and ⅓ of mozzarella cheese. Scatter with olive slices and sprinkle with Parmesan cheese. Bake at 425° to 450° until crust is brown and cheese is melted. 3 pies serve 6.

# CRAYFISH IN TEMPURA

(Goes nicely with Chawan Mushi)


EGG      1
ICE WATER      1 cup
SALT      ½ teaspoon
FLOUR      1 cup
CRAYFISH MEAT      1 cup firm pieces cooked and cleaned
VARIETY of FRESH VEGETABLES      2 cups
SUGGESTED VEGETABLES:
CARROTS      cut into ¼-inch strips
CAULIFLOWER FLOWERETS
GREEN PEPPER      cut into ¾-inch strips
GREEN ONION      cut into 2-inch lengths
MUSHROOM BUTTONS
SWEET POTATOES      sliced into ¼-inch slices
VEGETABLE OIL      enough for deep frying


Combine egg, water, and salt in mixing bowl. Add flour and beat well. Drop crayfish and vegetables into batter, 1 at a time. Be certain each piece is well coated. Preheat deep fat to 375° and deep fry for 1 minute on each side or until coating becomes golden brown. Drain on paper towels in warm oven. Serve hot. Serves 4.

# CHAWAN MUSHI

(This dish may be made using a wok fitted with a Chinese bamboo steamer with top. A roasting pan will also do nicely if it is fitted with a rack placed above the water level so that the food may be steamed.)

> EGGS      10
> SALT      1 tablespoon
> DRY SHERRY      2 tablespoons
> WATER      3 cups hot (not boiling)
> CRAYFISH MEAT      ¾ cup cooked and cleaned

Break eggs in mixing bowl and beat until foamy. Add salt and sherry. Gradually beat in water. Stir in finely chopped crayfish. Pour mixture into a round, 10-inch ovenproof glass or aluminum dish with a ½-inch border. Place dish in wok or pan over boiling water. Cover and steam 20 to 30 minutes or until a knife comes clean when testing. Serves 6 to 8.

# CRAWFISH MARGUÉRY

HOLLANDAISE-CRAWFISH SAUCE     see below
WATER     ½ cup
GREEN ONIONS     2, minced
FISH FILLETS     4 or
(FROZEN SCALLOPS     1 pound, steamed)
PARSLEY SPRIGS     4
EGGS     2, hard-cooked and sliced
PAPRIKA     sprinkle

Prepare Hollandaise-Crawfish Sauce and keep warm. Place water and green onions in saucepan over low heat. Add fish fillets and poach until flaky. Pour sauce over fillets. Garnish with parsley and eggs; sprinkle with paprika. Serves 4.


## HOLLANDAISE-CRAWFISH SAUCE

HOLLANDAISE SAUCE     1½ to 2 cups
CRAWFISH MEAT     1 cup cooked and cleaned
MUSHROOMS     1 4-ounce can, drained and chopped
BUTTER

Prepare hollandaise sauce or use prepared mix. Finely chop crawfish. Sauté mushrooms in butter. Add crawfish and mushrooms to sauce. Serves 4.

# CRAWFISH ÉTOUFFÉ

MARGARINE     ½ cup
MEDIUM ONIONS     6, finely chopped
CELERY     ½ cup chopped
TOMATO PASTE     ¼ teaspoon
CRAWFISH MEAT     4 cups cooked and cleaned
CORNSTARCH     ½ teaspoon
COLD WATER     ½ cup
SALT and PEPPER     to taste
CRUSHED RED PEPPER     to taste
GREEN ONION TOPS     ¼ cup minced
PARSLEY     ¼ cup minced
RICE     cooked

Put margarine, onions, celery, and tomato paste into heavy pot. Cook uncovered over medium heat until onions are transparent. Add crawfish meat. Dissolve cornstarch in cold water and add to crawfish, stirring constantly. Season to taste. Bring to a boil over medium heat and cook uncovered for 15 minutes. Stir in green onion tops and parsley. Serve over cooked rice. Serves 6 to 8.

.   .   .   .   .   .

There are over 500 species and subspecies of crawfish in the world. Over 250 of these species and subspecies can be found in North America.

# CRAWFISH PIE

(This recipe may look complicated, but it is really simple if taken step by step. The extra pies may be frozen for future use, which is an unusual bonus in any fish recipe.)

| | |
|---|---|
| PIE SHELLS | 12 |
| COOKING OIL | 1 cup |
| WHITE ONIONS | 2 cups chopped |
| CELERY | 1 cup chopped |
| GREEN PEPPER | 1 cup chopped |
| GARLIC CLOVES | 3 to 4, finely chopped |
| PEPPER | to taste |
| PAPRIKA | to taste |
| CRAWFISH FAT | from crawfish used in recipe |
| MEDIUM-SIZED GREEN ONION BOTTOMS | 1 bunch |
| CORNSTARCH | 4 tablespoons |
| WATER | 3 cups |
| GREEN ONION TOPS | 1 bunch, chopped |
| PARSLEY | ½ cup finely chopped |
| GARLIC CLOVES | 6, pressed or crushed |
| CRAWFISH TAILS | 4 pounds, cooked and cleaned |
| SALT | to taste |
| PASTRY | to cover pies |

Prepare pie shells in 16-ounce pyrex pie dishes; set aside. In oil, soften onions, celery, green pepper, and chopped garlic over medium heat. Sprinkle with pepper and paprika to taste. Add crawfish fat. Stir, cooking 10 minutes. Coarsely chop green onion bottoms; add ½ bunch. Cook 10 minutes. Mix cornstarch with water and gradually add to vegetables, stirring constantly. When thickened, add remaining green onions (tops and bottoms), parsley, and garlic, stirring constantly. Reduce heat and simmer 10 minutes. Season crawfish with black pepper; add crawfish. Season to taste with salt and pepper. Cool mixture slightly. Fill pie shells, leaving room for heat expansion during baking process. Cover tops with pastry. Slash vents for steam escape *unless* you plan to *freeze* pies. Bake at 350° for 15 minutes. Reduce heat to 300° and bake until tops and bottoms are golden brown. *To serve* place pies upside down on plates and tap inverted bottoms with spoon. *To freeze* cover unslit tops of pies with foil and place in freezer. One pie will furnish the main course for a hungry man.

.    .    .    .    .    .

There are twenty-nine known species of crawfish in Louisiana.

# CRAWFISH BISQUE

LIVE CRAWFISH    20 pounds
WATER    boiling
LARGE ONIONS    2
LARGE GREEN PEPPER    1
COOKING OIL    ½ cup
FLOUR    1 cup
WATER    4½ cups boiling
SALT    3 teaspoons
CRUSHED RED PEPPER    2 teaspoons
GREEN ONIONS    ½ cup chopped
PARSLEY    ½ cup finely chopped
CRAWFISH HEADS*    baked and stuffed

Wash crawfish. Drop crawfish into boiling water and cook until red. Separate heads from tails and save heads to fill with stuffing. Pour fat from heads into a dish. Clean crawfish. Divide tails and fat equally for bisque and stuffing. To make bisque, grind onions and green pepper. Make a golden brown roux with oil and flour. Add onion and green pepper to roux and cook until soft, stirring frequently. Add half the tail meat and crawfish fat and cook over low heat for about 20 minutes. Gradually add boiling water, salt, and red pepper and cook for another 20 mintues. Add green onions and parsley. Just before serving, add baked stuffed crawfish heads as a garnish. Serve with rice and crackers. Serves 10 generously.

*Baked crawfish heads recipe follows. Don't despair! You won't eat the heads! They are used only as small containers for a delicious stuffing.

# BAKED STUFFED CRAWFISH HEADS

(This stuffing is excellent in ramekins! Whichever you use, heads or ramekins, the stuffed "stuff" is served with bisque, either as a garnish or, if in ramekins, as a side dish.)

CRAWFISH HEADS     (from bisque recipe)
MEDIUM ONIONS     2
LARGE GREEN PEPPER     1
CRAWFISH TAILS     (from bisque recipe)
COOKING OIL     ¼ cup
FLOUR     ½ cup
CRAWFISH FAT     (from bisque recipe)
WATER     ¾ cup
SALT     1½ teaspoons
CRUSHED RED PEPPER     1½ teaspoons
BREAD CRUMBS     1½ cups
PARSLEY     ¼ cup finely chopped
GREEN ONION TOPS     ¼ cup finely chopped
BUTTER     ½ cup
FLOUR

Remove eyes and clean out heads of crawfish to be used as containers for stuffing. Grind onions and green pepper. Grind the remaining crawfish tail meat not used in bisque. Make a golden roux with oil and flour; add onion and green pepper and cook until soft. Add ground crawfish tails and remaining crawfish fat and simmer for 15 minutes. Add water, salt, and red pepper. Next add bread crumbs, parsley, and green onion; then add butter. Stir and allow butter to melt. Fill each head with stuffing, sprinkle with flour, and bake in a moderate oven for 15 minutes.

# CRAWFISH JAMBALAYA

BUTTER or MARGARINE     1 cup
FLOUR     2 tablespoons
MEDIUM ONIONS     6, chopped
CRAWFISH FAT     from crawfish being used
CRAWFISH TAIL MEAT     3 cups cooked and cleaned
PARSLEY     ¼ cup chopped
GREEN ONION TOPS     ¼ cup chopped
SALT and BLACK PEPPER     to taste
CRUSHED RED PEPPER     to taste
RICE     3 cups cooked, hot

Melt butter and add flour. Brown mix over medium heat. Add onions and simmer until soft; add crawfish fat.* Simmer a few more minutes and then add crawfish, parsley, green onion, and seasonings. Cook for 15 minutes over low heat. When ready to serve, mix with rice. Serves 6 to 8.

*The fat is used to give the dish bouquet.

. . . . .

Trapping: Trapping crawfish is probably the most expedient way to catch them. Crab pots that have been modified to hold crawfish or cylindrical traps made of hardware cloth are baited with fish heads or carcasses, chicken necks, meat, or cans of pet food into which holes have been punctured. Lowering the traps in the water, the crawfisherman waits a few hours and then brings the traps from the depths and places the catch in holding tanks.

# CRAWFISH GUMBO

OKRA      3 cups diced or
(FROZEN CUT OKRA      2 10-ounce boxes)
CELERY      ¾ cup chopped
GREEN PEPPER      1, chopped
GARLIC CLOVES      2, chopped
OIL      4 tablespoons
GREEN ONIONS      2 bunches, chopped
PARSLEY      2 tablespoons chopped
TOMATOES      1 16-ounce can
TOMATO SAUCE      1 8-ounce can
BAY LEAF      1, crumbled
THYME      ½ teaspoon
FILÉ*      ½ teaspoon, optional
SALT and PEPPER      to taste
CRAWFISH MEAT      3 cups cooked and cleaned or
(CRAWFISH MEAT      2 cups and
CRAB MEAT or LOBSTER MEAT      1 cup)
WATER      4 quarts
RICE      cooked

Sauté okra, celery, green pepper, and garlic in oil in heavy pot. Add green onions and parsley and cook 2 minutes longer. Add tomatoes and tomato sauce. Add spices. Cook over medium heat 20 minutes. Add crawfish and 3 quarts water. Cook for 30 minutes. Add 1 more quart water. Simmer covered for 1 hour over low heat. Serve over rice in soup bowls. Serves 6 to 8.

*Filé: powdered young leaves of sassafras.

.   .   .   .   .   .

Gumbo is a Creole favorite and was originated by the gourmets of New Orleans. Combinations of seafoods and chicken can be used. Gumbo should never be reheated if filé is used in the seasoning, as boiling will tend to make it stringy. The customary way to serve gumbo is from a tureen heated in a bain-marie, or in some other hot water bath.

# FAST JAMBALAYA

| | |
|---|---|
| BACON | 4 thick slices, diced |
| CELERY | ½ cup chopped |
| SPANISH RICE DINNER | 1 6-ounce package |
| TOMATO SAUCE | 1 15-ounce can |
| CRAWFISH MEAT | 1 cup cooked and cleaned |
| PARSLEY | minced, to garnish |

Fry bacon crisp in 10-inch skillet; remove bacon and drain. Cook celery in drippings until tender; drain fat. Follow directions on package of Spanish rice dinner but use tomato sauce instead of amount of water called for. Stir in crawfish and celery. Simmer uncovered for 5 minutes. Garnish with parsley and bacon. Serves 6.

# CRAWFISH CREOLE

ONION      ½ cup chopped
CELERY      ½ cup chopped
GREEN PEPPER      ½ cup chopped
GARLIC CLOVE      1, minced
BUTTER      ⅓ cup, melted
SALT      1 teaspoon
PEPPER      ¼ teaspoon
CAYENNE      dash
BAY LEAF      1, crushed
FLOUR      2 tablespoons
SUGAR      1 teaspoon
TOMATOES      2 1-pound, 4-ounce cans
CRAWFISH      50, cooked, shelled, and cleaned
RICE      3 cups cooked
PARSLEY      ¼ cup chopped

Sauté onion, celery, green pepper, and garlic in butter until tender. Add seasonings. Stir in flour, sugar, and tomatoes. Bring to a boil. Reduce heat and cook for 20 minutes. Add crawfish meat. Cover and cook slowly 10 to 15 minutes. Serve over rice. Garnish with parsley. Serves 6 to 8.

.   .   .   .   .   .

To catch a crawfish by the casual method, turn over rocks and logs in a stream and grab them behind the front claws—they'll pinch if you get ahead of them! You can also use a long-handled net to catch them. Remember, they scuttle fast in forward and swim fast in reverse.

# BAKED CRAWFISH JAMBALAYA

ONION     ½ cup chopped
BUTTER     2 tablespoons
GARLIC CLOVE     1, crushed
CRAWFISH MEAT     1 cup or more cooked and cleaned
TOMATOES     1 1-pound can
CANNED CONDENSED CHICKEN BROTH     ¾ cup or
(BOUILLON CUBES     2, dissolved in ¾ cup hot WATER)
PARSLEY     1 tablespoon chopped
BAY LEAF     1
SALT     1 teaspoon
THYME     ¼ teaspoon
TABASCO SAUCE     ½ teaspoon
PEPPER     ⅛ teaspoon
LONG-GRAINED WHITE RICE     1 cup

Sauté onion in butter until soft. Add garlic and crawfish meat. Sauté 5 minutes longer. Stir in tomatoes, chicken broth, parsley, bay leaf, salt, and thyme. Add Tabasco and pepper. Cover and bring to a boil. Pour into greased 2-quart casserole. Sprinkle uncooked rice over top of mixture; press rice into mixture so as to cover rice with liquid. *Do not stir!* Cover casserole. Bake at 350° for 40 minutes or until rice is tender and liquid is absorbed. Serves 6.

This is the way my friend, Thomas Reed, says they have a "crawfish feed" in Louisiana. His family lives there, so Thomas should know all about it!

"You get a gunnysack of crawfish and plan for enough of them to fill everybody up. Then you build a good deep fire with a big old iron pot hanging over it by a chain.

"Dump the crawfish into a washtub so you can check them over to make sure they're alive. Meanwhile, put your spices [pickling spice is fine], cut-up lemons, and salt in the water and let it boil hard. [*Again, the ratio of salt to water is ½ cup salt to 1 gallon water.*] Then throw green onions and scrubbed potatoes [either small whole ones or cut-up big ones] into the pot.

"When the pot is boiling again, dump in the crawfish and cook them until they're done. [Clean before eating.]

"What do you serve with them? You don't need anything more to eat than that! With cold beer to drink, everybody has plenty!"

Thomas added, "Louisiana crawfish are bigger than northern ones and seem to have smaller claws."

*The following recipes are awfully good side dishes for crawfish.*

# HUSH PUPPIES

(Authentic Louisiana recipe)

FLOUR      ½ cup sifted
CORNMEAL      1 cup
ONION      1, minced
BAKING POWDER      1½ teaspoons
EGG      1
SALT      1 teaspoon
SUGAR      1 teaspoon
MILK      as needed
COOKING OIL

Mix first 7 ingredients with just enough milk to moisten dough to a stiff consistency but soft enough to spoon. Dip with a tablespoon and drop into hot deep fat (350°). Cook until golden brown. Makes about 18 pups.

# GRITS SOUFFLÉ

(Authentic southern dish)

GRITS    1 cup, cooked
BUTTER    ½ cup
SHARP CHEESE    3 6-ounce packages, chopped
GARLIC CHEESE    1 6-ounce package, chopped
EGGS    3, separated
WORCESTERSHIRE SAUCE    to taste
SALT    1 teaspoon
GARLIC SALT    to taste

To the hot grits add butter, cheeses, beaten egg yolks, Worcestershire, and seasonings. Mix until cheese melts. Fold in stiffly beaten egg whites. Put into ungreased casserole. Bake 30 minutes at 300°. Serve within 20 minutes. Makes 4 quarts. Stores well for later serving.

# DIRTY RICE

(An authentic recipe from Louisiana, served with boiled crawfish)

PORK ROAST      3 or 4 pounds
WATER      as needed
LARGE ONION      1, chopped
GREEN ONION TOPS      4
RICE      3 cups cooked
PARSLEY      chopped, to garnish

Finely grind or chop roast. Brown slowly in heavy pan, adding small amount of water as needed. Add onion and cook until onion is tender. Add green onion and cook for about 2 minutes. Add rice to pork mixture. Garnish with parsley. Serves 6 to 8.

# RED BEANS AND RICE

| | |
|---|---|
| RED BEANS | 1 pound |
| BACON DRIPPINGS | 1 tablespoon |
| HAM HOCK | 1 |
| LARGE ONIONS | 2, chopped |
| GARLIC CLOVES | 2, minced |
| SALT | 1 teaspoon |
| BLACK PEPPER | ½ teaspoon |
| RED PEPPER | ¼, crushed |
| WATER | 4 cups |
| RICE | cooked |

Wash beans. Soak overnight. Drain. Heat bacon drippings in heavy pot. Add ham hock. Sauté to render more drippings (about 10 minutes). Remove hock. Stir in onions and garlic. Sauté 5 minutes; then add beans, seasonings, and ham hock. Add water and bring to a boil. Place cover on pot and lower heat to simmer about 6 hours. Stir frequently during last 2 hours of cooking. Serve with hot rice. Serves 6.

# RIVER HOUSE SPECIAL GRITS

"QUICK" GRITS     1½ cups
WATER     6 cups
PASTEURIZED PROCESSED CHEESE     1 pound, cut into bits
BUTTER     ¾ cup
TABASCO SAUCE     11 shakes
EGGS     3

Cook grits in water. Remove from stove and add cheese. Add butter and Tabasco sauce. Beat in eggs. Bake in greased casserole for 1 hour at 375°. Serves 12, generously. This recipe can be made a day ahead and refrigerated until time to bake.

# Index

Appetizers/Cocktails
  Crawfish Chunks   29
  Crawfish Cocktail   24
  Crawfish in Court Bouillon   27
  Crawfish Party Dip   28
  Eggs Stuffed with Crawfish   31
  Fried Crawfish Cakes (balls)   111
  Marinated Crawfish   26
  Mock *Mousse de Crevettes*   30
  Smoked Crawfish   25
  Toasty Crawfish Appetizer   28
Boiling Crawfish   15
  Louisiana Crawfish Feed   143
  Methods I through IX   16-20
Casseroles
  Chicken and Crawfish Casserole   83
  Company Crawfish   97
  Crawdads 'n' Rice   86
  Crawfish and Artichokes   89
  Crawfish Cheese Bake   87
  Crawfish de Jonghe   90
  Crawfish Duchesse   78
  Crawfish Fondue   88
  Crawfish Harpin Casserole   99
  Crawfish Mushroom Casserole   96
  Crawfish Puffs   85
  Crawfish Sorrento   95
  Crawfish Tetrazzini   84
  Crusty Crawfish   79
  Deviled Crawfish   80
  Fast Crawfish Curry   82
  Helyn's Casserole   81
  Oodles of Noodles and 'Dads   94
  Quick Crawfish Curry Casserole   100
  River House Supper   93
  Scappoose Crawfish and
    Crab Special   92
  Tomato-Crawfish Bake   98

  Weird and Wonderful Casserole   91
Cleaning crawfish   11
Cocktail Sauces and Dressings
  A Very Delicate Sauce   35
  *Beurre Blanc*   39
  Crawfish Sauce   36
  Cream Crawfish Dressing   58
  Creole Cocktail Sauce   33
  Curry Dressing   64
  Drawn Butter Sauce   35
  Family Favorite   32
  Louis Dressing   63
  *Maître d'Hôtel* Butter   37
  Mustard Butter   37
  Pink Mayonnaise   38
  River House Crawfish Dressing   32
  Rocky Point Sauce   34
  Sauvie Island Salad Dressing   59
  Tart Cocktail Sauce   34
  White Wine Dressing   50
Crawfish fat   13
Crêpes
  Dinner Crêpes   72
  Luncheon Crêpes   73
Deep South Specials   121
  Dirty Rice   146
  Grits Soufflé   145
  Hush Puppies   144
  Louisiana Crawfish Feed   143
  Red Beans and Rice   147
  River House Special Grits   148
Dressings. *See* Cocktail Sauces
    and Dressings
Entrées
  Crawfish Avocado   104
  Crawfish Boats   115
  Crawfish in Lemon Butter   105
  Crawfish in Patty Shells   109

Crawfish in Sour Cream   106
Crawfish Newburg   113
Crawfish Stuffed Peppers   118
Crawfish Wiggle   110
Curried Crawfish   112
Deep-Fried Crawfish   107
Easy Crawfish Thermidor   114
Fried Crawfish Cakes   111
Kim and Dan's Easy Elegance   117
Oven-Fried Crawfish   116
Tomatoes Stuffed with Crawfish   108
See also Casseroles
   Entrées (International)
   Entrées (Southern)
Entrées (International)
   Chawan Mushi   131
   Chinese Crawfish Dinner   125
   Crawdad Tacos II   127
   Crawfish Fricassee   122
   Crawfish Italienne   124
   Crawfish Marguéry   132
   Crawfish Pizza   129
   Crawfish Tacos I   126
   Crayfish in Tempura   130
   Creamy Herbal Crawfish   123
   Sweet and Sour Crawfish   128
Entrées (Southern)
   Baked Crawfish Jambalaya   142
   Baked Stuffed Crawfish Heads   137
   Crawfish Bisque   136
   Crawfish Creole   141
   Crawfish Étouffé   133
   Crawfish Gumbo   139
   Crawfish Jambalaya   138
   Crawfish Pie   134
   Fast Jambalaya   140
   Louisiana Crawfish Feed   143
Quiches
   Crawdad Quiche   75
   Curried Crawfish Quiche   74
Salads
   Broiled Tomato-Crawfish Salad   58
   Cold Crawfish Salad   50
   Crawfish and Cucumber
      Quickie Salad   53

Crawfish Arnaud   54
Crawfish Cruising Salad   56
Crawfish Louis   63
Crawfish Remoulade   61
Fruited Seafood Salad   64
Houseboat Supper Salad   52
Overnight Party Salad   62
Provençale Crawfish Salad   51
Rocky Point Bean
   and Crawfish Salad   55
Sauvie Island Salad   59
Sliced Tomato Crawfish   60
Sunday Night Salad   49
Willamette River Salad   57
Sandwiches
   Crawfish Picnic Patties   68
   Hot and Cheesy Crawdad Rolls   66
   Jessie's Crawfish Rolls   65
   Open-faced Crawfish-
      and-Cheese Sandwich   67
Sauces
   Dinner Crêpes Topping   72
   Hollandaise-Crawfish Sauce   132
   See also Cocktail Sauces
      and Dressings   23
Side Dishes for Crawfish. See Deep
   South Specials
Soups/Chowders
   Columbia River Bouillabaisse   48
   Crawdad Soup for Summer   43
   Crawfish Bisque Manchac   47
   Crawfish Chowder   44
   Crawfish Stew I   45
   Crawfish Stew II   46
   Multnomah Channel Chowder   42
Stews. See Soups/Chowders

# OTHER PAPERBACKS FROM PACIFIC SEARCH PRESS

## COOKING

*Asparagus: The Sparrowgrass Cookbook* by Autumn Stanley. Over 100 ways to serve the low-calorie, nutritious vegetable of kings with helpful tips on cultivation. Drawings. 160 pp. $3.95.

*Bone Appétit! Natural Foods for Pets* by Frances Sheridan Goulart. Treat your pet to some home-cooked meals made only with pure, natural ingredients. Recipes fit for both man and beast! Drawings. 96 pp. $2.95.

*The Carrot Cookbook* by Ann Saling. Over 200 mouth-watering recipes. Drawings. 160 pp. $3.50.

*The Dogfish Cookbook* by Russ Mohney. Over 65 piscine delights. Cartoons and drawings. 108 pp. $1.95.

*The Green Tomato Cookbook* by Paula Simmons. More than 80 solutions to the bumper crop. 96 pp. $2.95.

*Wild Mushroom Recipes* by the Puget Sound Mycological Society. 2d edition. Over 200 recipes. 176 pp. $6.95.

*The Zucchini Cookbook* by Paula Simmons. Revised and enlarged 2d edition. Over 150 tasty creations. 160 pp. $3.50.

## NATURE

*Butterflies Afield in the Pacific Northwest* by William Neill/Douglas Hepburn, photography. Lovely guide with 74 unusual color photos of living butterflies. 96 pp. $5.95.

*Cascade Companion* by Susan Schwartz/Bob and Ira Spring, photography. Nature and history of the Washington Cascades. Black-and-white photos, maps. 160 pp. $5.95.

*Common Seaweeds of the Pacific Coast* by J. Robert Waaland. Introduction to the world of the seaweed—its biology, conservation, and many uses to both industry and seafood lovers. 42 color photos, diagrams, illustrations. 128 pp. $5.95.

*Fire and Ice: The Cascade Volcanoes* by Stephen L. Harris. Copublished with the Mountaineers. Black-and-white photos and drawings, maps. 320 pp. $7.95.

*Little Mammals of the Pacific Northwest* by Ellen Kritzman. The only book of its kind devoted solely to the Northwest's little mammals. 48 color and black-and-white photos, distribution maps, index. 128 pp. $5.95.

*Living Shores of the Pacific Northwest* by Lynwood Smith/Bernard Nist, photography. Fascinating guide to seashore life. Over 140 photos, 110 in color. 160 pp. $9.95.

*Minnie Rose Lovgreen's Recipe for Raising Chickens* by Minnie Rose Lovgreen. 2d edition. 32 pp. $2.00.

*Sleek & Savage: North America's Weasel Family* by Delphine Haley. Extraordinary color and black-and-white photos; bibliography. 128 pp. $5.50.

*Why Wild Edibles? The Joys of Finding, Fixing, and Tasting—West of the Rockies* by Russ Mohney. Color and black-and-white photos, illustrations. 320 pp. $6.95.